Taunton's
BUILD LIKE A PRO®
Expert Advice from Start to Finish

BUILDING KITCHEN
CABINETS

BUILD LIKE A PRO®

BUILDING KITCHEN CABINETS

UDO SCHMIDT

The Taunton Press

The Taunton Press
Inspiration for hands-on living®

The Taunton Press, Inc., 63 South Main Street, P.O. Box 5506, Newtown, CT 06470-5506
e-mail: tp@taunton.com

EDITOR: Tim Snyder
COVER AND INTERIOR DESIGN: Lori Wendin
LAYOUT: Jeff Potter and Paul Rydzewski/Potter Publishing Studio
ILLUSTRATOR: Ron Carboni
PHOTOGRAPHS: ©Thomas Feagin: pp. ii, iii, v, vi (2, 3, 4, 5), 1 (6, 7, 9, 10), 2, 3, 6, 7, 8, 9, 10 (bottom left and right), 11, 12, 13, 14, 15, 16, 17, 18, 19 (1, 2), 20, 21, 22 (bottom), 23, 24, 25, 26, 30, 31 (3, 4), 34, 35, 38, 39 (top), 41, 42, 43, 44 (bottom), 46, 47, 48 (bottom), 49 (right), 54, 55, 56, 61, 62, 63 (bottom left and right), 64, 65, 66, 67, 69, 70, 71, 74, 75, 78 (top), 79, 80 (top left and right, bottom right), 81 (top), 82 (top left and right, bottom right), 83, 84, 85 (2, 3, 5), 88, 90, 91, 94, 95, 97 (2, 3, 5), 100, 101, 102, 105, 107 (2, 4), 109 (left), 111, 112, 113, 114, 115, 117 (top), 118 (bottom), 120 (right), 121, 122, 123 (2, 3), 124, 126, 127 (bottom), 128 (middle), 129, 130, 131, 134, 135 (1, 2, 3, 4), 136 (bottom middle and right), 137, 138 (top right, bottom right), 139, 140 (top right, bottom right), 141, 142, 144, 145, 146, 147, 149, 150, 151, 152, 153, 154, 155 (1, 2, 3, 4, 6), 156, 157, 158, 159, 160, 161, 162 (top), 163 (top). © Udo Schmidt: pp. vi (1), 1 (8), 10 (top), 27, 31 (1), 39 (bottom), 40, 44 (top), 48 (left), 49 (left), 51, 52, 53, 63 (top), 78 (bottom), 80 (bottom left), 81 (bottom), 82 (bottom), 85 (1, 4), 89, 92, 93, 96, 97 (1, 4), 103, 106, 107 (1, 3, 5), 108, 109 (right), 110 (bottom), 116, 117 (bottom), 118 (left), 119, 120 (left), 123 (1, 4), 125, 127 (top and middle), 128 (top and bottom), 132, 133, 135 (5, 6), 136 (left), 138 (top and bottom left), 140 (left), 143 (bottom), 155 (5), 162 (left). ©The Taunton Press: pp. 22 (*Fine Homebuilding* #120, p. 138) courtesy of Mt. Baker Plywood, 28 (top) (*Understanding Wood*, p. 246) courtesy of Vincent Laurance (bottom) (*Fine Woodworking* #151, p. 75) courtesy of Michael Pekovich, 29 (*Understanding Wood*, p. 146) courtesy of Bruce Hoadley, 34 (left) courtesy of Scott Phillips, 163 (bottom) (*Fine Homebuilding* #143, p. 45) courtesy of Charles Miller.

LIBRARY OF CONGRESS CATALOGING-IN-PUBLICATION DATA
Schmidt, Udo.
  Building kitchen cabinets : expert advice from start to finish / Udo Schmidt.
      p. cm. – (Taunton's build like a pro)
ISBN-13: 978-1-56158-470-3
ISBN-10: 1-56158-470-3
1. Kitchen cabinets. 2. Cabinetwork. I. Title. II. Series
  TT197.5.K57 S347 2002
    684.1'6–dc21
                          2002152497
Printed in the United States of America
10 9 8 7 6 5

About Your Safety: Home building is inherently dangerous. Using hand or power tools improperly or ignoring safety practices can lead to permanent injury or even death. Don't try to perform operations you learn about here (or elsewhere), unless you're certain they are safe for you. If something about an operation doesn't feel right, don't do it. Look for another way. We want you to enjoy the craft, so please keep safety foremost in your mind whenever you're in the shop.

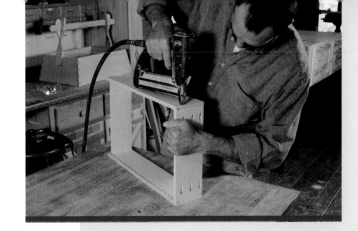

To my wife, Tere: her support, encouragement, and love made me see this project through.

Acknowledgments

My appreciation goes to Tom Clark, who got me started writing this book. Many thanks also go to Tim Snyder, whose skillful editing organized and polished the text.

Most of the images were photographed by Tom Fagin, who patiently waited for me to build the kitchen cabinets for this book so he could get various shots.

I also thank my fellow cabinetmakers Joe Morgan and Marc Morgan for their willingness to help and for their invaluable trade information. David Cornell also gave me great inside information on finishing.

Buddy Pulliam and Chris Carpenter were always ready to help when I needed information on materials and hardware.

Many thanks go to my customers who opened their homes for us to take photos, especially Marc and Jan Sharp, Jerry and Julie Millican, Alden and Nancy Schaffer, Denis and Terry Stamey, and John and Lucy Meggett.

Finally, a book like this is not possible without the many people who work behind the scenes in the publishing field. My special thanks go to those whose names don't appear in the credits.

Contents

Introduction 3

How to Use This Book 4

■ CHAPTER ONE

Tools 6

First, a Table Saw 8

Other Stationary Machinery 10

Portable Power Tools and Accessories 13

Other Tools and Equipment 17

■ CHAPTER TWO

Understanding Wood 18

Composite-Wood Panels 20

Solid Wood 24

Sources for Lumber 27

■ CHAPTER THREE

Design 30

Design Ideas 32

Making Drawings 32

Doors and Drawers 37

Designing Custom Cabinets 39

■ CHAPTER FOUR

Face-Frame Construction 42

Dimensioning Face Frames 44

Assembling Face Frames 47

■ CHAPTER FIVE

Doors and Panels 54

Door Design Options 56

Calculating and Cutting Door Parts 58

Milling Door Parts 61

Assembling Doors 67

Building End Panels 71

■ CHAPTER SIX

Building Drawers 74

Style, Joinery, and Materials 76

Building a Basic Drawer Box 78

Building a Dovetailed Drawer 81

Making Drawer Fronts 83

■ CHAPTER SEVEN

Base Cabinets 84

Making a Cutlist 86

Cutting Panels to Size 87

Assembling Standard Base Cabinets 87

Building Corner Base Cabinets 91

Building End Panel Cabinets 94

■ CHAPTER EIGHT

Wall Cabinets 96

Dimensions and Design Options 98

Cutting and Joinery Details 98

Assembling Standard Wall Cabinets 101

Building End Panel Cabinets 103

Building Corner Wall Cabinets 104

■ CHAPTER NINE

Other Cabinets 106

Wall Cabinets above the Stove 108

Refrigerator Cabinets 108

Cabinets for Wall Ovens 109

Pantry Cabinets 110

Island Cabinets 110

■ CHAPTER TEN

Finishing 112

Sanding and Surface Preparation 114

Choosing a Finish 115

Using Paint and Stain 121

■ CHAPTER ELEVEN

Hardware 122

Concealed Hinges 124

Drawer-Slide Hardware 128

Knobs and Pulls 131

Attaching Drawer Fronts 132

■ CHAPTER TWELVE

Accessories 134

Shelves and Shelf Supports 136

Sink Trays 140

Trash Doors 141

Rollout Shelves 142

Lazy Susans 142

Appliance Garages 143

■ CHAPTER THIRTEEN

Installation 144

Plumb, Level, and Square 146

Shimming, Scribing, and Trimming 147

Installing Wall Cabinets 149

Installing Base Cabinets 150

Crown Molding and Kickspace Trim 151

■ CHAPTER FOURTEEN

Countertops 154

Plastic Laminate 156

Solid Surface Material and Engineered Stone 156

Granite and Soapstone 160

Tile 161

Solid Wood 162

Installing Countertops 162

Resources 165

Index 167

Introduction

BUILDING AN entire kitchen's worth of cabinets is a large-scale woodworking project. When you imagine a 30-ft. expanse of continuous cabinetry, it's no wonder many woodworkers develop a mental block about building kitchen cabinets. And it's easy to justify this resistance by arguing that major cabinet manufacturers now offer a seemingly endless variety of choices when it comes to cabinetry styles, wood species, finishes, and special accessories.

But neither the scale of the project nor the capabilities of cabinet manufacturers should dissuade you from designing and building your own cabinets from scratch. It's true that a kitchen full of cabinets represents a great deal of lumber and plenty of joinery work. But you use the same construction techniques on one cabinet as you do on many. This book will show you how joinery and assembly work can be simplified without sacrificing a cabinet's quality or appearance. To succeed as a professional cabinetmaker, this knowledge is critical. If you put my techniques to work in your own shop, you'll be surprised at how quickly you can build cabinets.

Limited space is a problem in many shops, including my own. But as you'll see in the pages ahead, the construction sequence I use calls for building the smaller components first—cabinet face frames, then doors and drawers. The cases, which take up the most space, are built at the end.

Although cabinet manufacturers have many "custom" options for customers to consider, they

can't compete with the details you can incorporate into your own custom-built cabinets. You can take extra time in selecting individual boards from which to make doors and drawer fronts. You can even utilize locally milled lumber or unusual wood that isn't available to large-scale manufacturers. Where factory-made cabinets show hardwood plywood, you can build a beautiful frame-and-panel assembly from solid wood. This book will also show you how to make curved-top and glass-paneled doors, as well as angled corners to replace standard right-angled corners. When you build your own cabinets, you're not limited by the standard dimensions that manufacturers use. Custom-sized pantry and island cabinets are no problem. You'll have the ability to do what your customers or your imagination suggests. Work safely, and good luck.

How to Use This Book

I F YOU'RE READING THIS, you're a doer who is not afraid to take on a challenging project. We've designed this book and this series to help you do that project smoothly and cost effectively.

Many doers jump in and do, reading the directions only if something goes wrong. It's much smarter (and cheaper) to start by knowing what to do and planning the process step by step. This book is here to help you. Read it. Familiarize yourself with the process you're about to undertake. You'll be glad you did.

Planning Is the Key to Success

This book contains information on designing your project, choosing the best options for the results you want to achieve, and planning the timing and execution. We know you're anxious to get started on your project. Take the time now to read and think about what you're about to do. You'll refine your ideas and choose the best materials.

There's advice here on where to look for inspiration and how to make plans. Don't be afraid to attempt drawing your own plans. There's no better way to get exactly what you want than by design-

ing it yourself. If you need the assistance of an architect or engineer, that part of the book will explain why and how to work with those professionals.

After you've decided what you're going to undertake, make lists of materials and a budget for yourself, both of money and of time. There's nothing more annoying than a project that goes on forever.

Finding the Information You Need

We've designed this book to make it easy to find what you need to know. The main part of the book details the essential parts of each process. If it's fairly straightforward, it's simply described. If there are key steps, they are addressed one by one, usually accompanied by drawings or photos to help you see what you will be doing. We've also added some other elements to help you understand the process better, find quicker or smarter ways to accomplish the task, or do it differently to suit your project.

Alternatives and a closer look

The sidebars and features included with the main text are there to explain aspects in more depth and to clarify why you're doing something. In some cases, they are used to describe a completely different way to handle the same situation. We explain when you may want to use that method or choose that option, as well as detail its advantages. The sidebars are usually accompanied by photos or drawings to help you see what the author is describing. The sidebars are meant to help, but they're not essential to understanding or doing the process.

Heads up!

We urge you to read the "Safety First" sidebars we've included. "Safety First" gives you a warning about hazards that can harm or even kill you. Always work safely. Use appropriate safety aids and know what you're doing before you start working. Don't take unnecessary chances, and if a procedure makes you uncomfortable, try to find another way to do it.

There's a pro at your elbow

The author of this book, and every author in this series, has had years of experience doing this kind of project. We've put the benefits of their knowledge into quick tips that always appear in the left margin. "Pro Tips" are ideas or insights that will save you time or money. "In Detail" is a short explanation of an aspect that may be of interest to you. While not essential to doing the job, it is meant to explain the "why."

Every project has its surprises. Since the author has encountered many of them already, he can give you a little preview of what they may be and how to address them. And experience has also taught the author some tricks that you can only learn from being a pro. Some of these are tips, some are tools or accessories you can make yourself, and some are materials or tools you may not have thought to use.

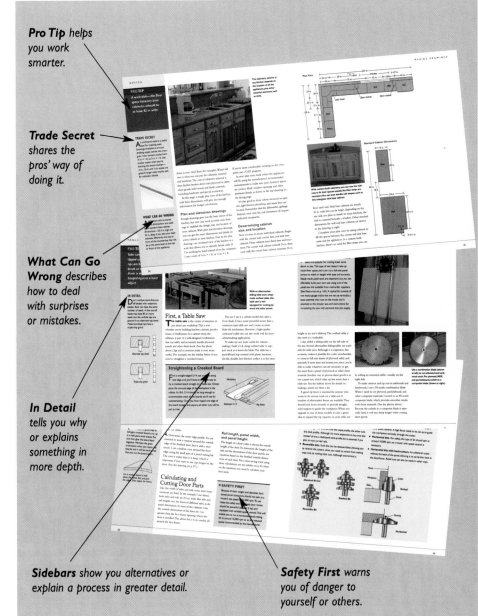

Pro Tip helps you work smarter.

Trade Secret shares the pros' way of doing it.

What Can Go Wrong describes how to deal with surprises or mistakes.

In Detail tells you why or explains something in more depth.

Sidebars show you alternatives or explain a process in greater detail.

Safety First warns you of danger to yourself or others.

Building Like a Pro

To make a living, a pro needs to work smart, quickly, and economically. That's the strategy presented in this book. We've provided options to help you make the best choices in design, materials, and methods. That way, you can adjust your project to suit your skill level and budget. Good choices and good planning are the keys to success. And remember that all the knowledge and every skill you acquire on this project will make the next project easier.

Tools

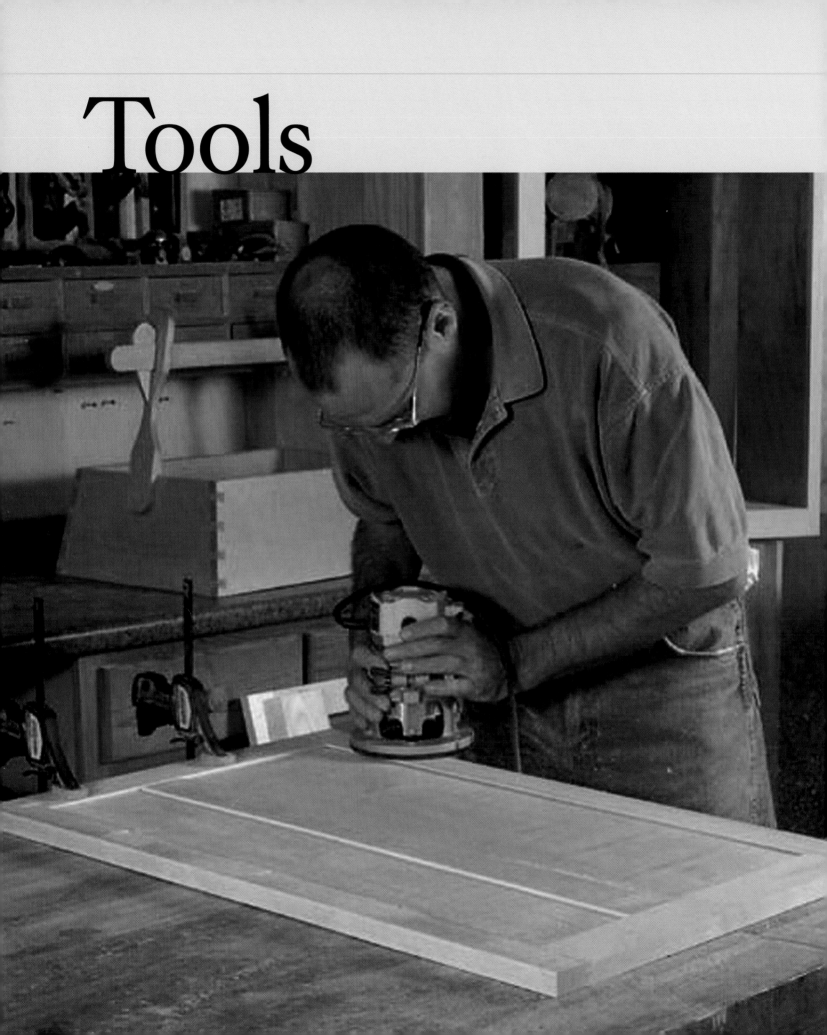

CHAPTER ONE

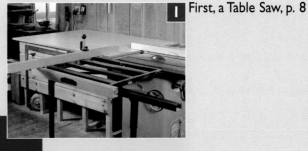

1 First, a Table Saw, p. 8

E ntire books have been written about the tools used by cabinetmakers and woodworkers. But if you're ready to learn about building kitchen cabinets, you already know quite a bit about this subject. In this chapter, I'll cover the tools and accessories that I rely on to build beautiful cabinets with a high degree of efficiency.

2 Other Stationary Machinery, p. 10

Whether you are a professional woodworker like me or a serious amateur, it's important to buy the best tools you can afford. Price and quality can vary greatly within a given tool category. If you're uncertain about what model or manufacturer is best for you, take the time to get advice from experienced woodworkers, either online or in your own neighborhood. Acquiring a new tool or accessory is exciting when you know it will help you save time, achieve better results, or do both. To work safely, make sure you follow the guidelines on p. 16.

3 Portable Power Tools and Accessories, p. 13

4 Other Tools and Equipment, p. 17

IN DETAIL

Don't confuse extra-fine cut-off blades with melamine blades. Both can have the same number of teeth. A fine cut-off blade may have 80 or more teeth, but the carbide tips are ground in an alternate top bevel. Melamine blade tips have a triple-chip grind.

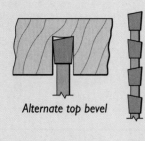

Alternate top bevel

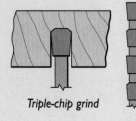

Triple-chip grind

With an aftermarket sliding table and a shop-made outfeed table, this table saw is well equipped for cutting plywood and other panels.

First, a Table Saw

The table saw is the center of attention in just about any workshop. This is true whether you're building kitchen cabinets, jewelry boxes, or birdhouses. In a cabinet shop, the tablesaw is part of a well-designed workstation that can safely and accurately handle plywood panels and other sheet stock. (See the photo above.) Jigs and accessories make it even more useful. (For example, see the sidebar below if you need to straighten a crooked board.)

The saw I use is a cabinet model that takes a 10-in. blade. It has a more powerful motor than a contractor-type table saw and a more accurate blade-tilt mechanism. However, a high-quality contractor's table saw can also work well for most cabinetmaking applications.

To make my saw more useful for cabinetmaking, I built a 6-ft.-long outfeed table to support stock as it leaves the blade. The table has a particleboard top covered with plastic laminate; this flat, durable, low-friction surface is at the same

Straightening a Crooked Board

Find a straight-edged 2×4, cut a rabbet along one edge, and you'll have an effective way to rip a crooked board straight on a table saw. Always place the concave edge of the workpiece in the rabbet. An 8-ft. 2×4 should be long enough to accommodate most of the boards you'll use for cabinetmaking. Once you have ripped one edge of the board straight and square, all other cuts will be just as true.

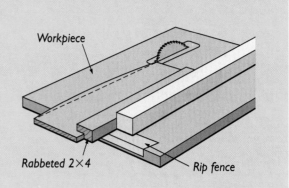

Workpiece

Rabbeted 2×4

Rip fence

Building Your Own Panel Saw

At lumberyards and large cabinet shops, panel saws are popular for cutting sheet stock down to size. This type of saw doesn't take up much floor space, yet it can cut a full-size panel across its width or length with ease and accuracy. Ready-made panel saws are expensive, but you can affordably build your own saw using one of the panel-saw kits available from mail-order suppliers. (See Resources on p. 165.) A typical kit consists of two heavy-gauge tracks that are set up vertically, a base assembly that runs on the tracks and is attached to the circular saw, and instructions for completing the saw with plywood that you supply.

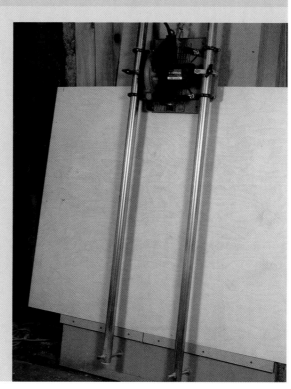

height as my saw's tabletop. The outfeed table is also used as a worktable.

I also added a sliding table on the left side of the saw. Several aftermarket sliding tables are available for table saws. Although it is expensive, this accessory makes it possible for a solo woodworker to crosscut full-size sheets of plywood safely and precisely. It saves time and money, too, since you're able to make whatever cuts are necessary to get the most from a panel of plywood or other sheet material. Another way to process sheet goods is to use a panel saw, which takes up less room than a table saw. See the sidebar above for details on making a panel saw from a kit.

A good rip fence is essential for anyone who wants to do serious work on a table saw. A number of aftermarket fences are available. They should lock down securely to provide straight, solid support to guide the workpiece. When you upgrade to one of those models, it's also a good idea to expand the rip capacity on your table saw

Use a combination blade (shown at left) to cut softwood and hardwood stock. For plywood, MDF, and particleboard, switch to a composite blade (shown at right).

by adding an extension table—usually on the right side.

To make crosscut and rip cuts in softwoods and hardwoods, I use a 50-tooth combination blade. When I need to cut plywood, particleboard, and other composite materials, I switch to an 80-tooth composite blade, which provides smoother results with those materials. (See the photos above.) Because the carbide in a composite blade is especially hard, it will stay sharp longer when cutting sheet goods.

TRADE SECRET

When a saw blade seems dull or out of balance, it might just need a good cleaning. Gunk that builds up around the carbide tips will cause the blade to cut poorly and can even make the blade vibrate because it's out of balance. To clean a blade, generously apply some oven cleaner to the carbide tips and let it soak for 15 minutes. Then use an old toothbrush to scrub the blade clean. Rinse with plenty of water and dry the blade thoroughly to prevent rust. I also coat the blade with a film of lubricant, such as WD-40. You will be surprised how much better a blade can cut after this treatment.

With a jointer, you can transform an irregular edge into one that's straight and square. It's also good for planing cupped boards flat.

Other Stationary Machinery

These are the big ticket items and the real workhorses in your shop. Although not all of these tools are essential, they definitely make it possible for you to be more productive and work more accurately. If you're not in a hurry to get your shop set up, you may want to scan local newspaper ads for good deals on used machinery. When good-quality machines are well cared for, they work just like new models but cost much less.

Jointer

A jointer can be very useful for all kinds of woodworking projects, but it's not absolutely essential for making cabinets, especially if the lumber you buy is flat and has at least one straight edge. If you are buying roughsawn stock or boards with wavy edges, you'll need this machine to plane surfaces flat and smooth and transform irregular edges into straight ones.

When you need to glue up a number of wide panels from narrower boards, a jointer gives you the straight, square edges that these glue-ups require. (See the photo above.) Skilled woodworkers can do this work with handplanes, but such a traditional approach takes too long when you're building a room full of cabinets.

The cutterhead on a thickness planer shaves wood from the top of the workpiece, leaving a smooth, flat surface. This machine earns its keep by planing parts to a uniform width and thickness.

Thickness planer

A thickness planer is essential for cabinetmaking. (See the photo at bottom photo on the facing page.) Even when you buy a load of preplaned lumber, you will certainly find that the surface on some boards is not as smooth as you would like and that the boards are not a uniform thickness. The planer solves both problems. As the planer's feed rollers pull a board across the bed of the machine, the cutterhead spins two or three knives at a high r.p.m., slicing off a thin layer of wood.

The portable planers available from major manufacturers, such as Delta®, DeWalt®, Makita®, and Rigid®, can handle boards that are 12 in. to 13 in. wide. These machines are affordable and do excellent smoothing and thicknessing work in a small-scale woodworking shop. I use my planer not only for thicknessing but also for planing face-frame stock to a uniform width by running the boards on edge through the machine.

Drill press

A drill press is one of the most versatile tools in the woodshop. I don't know of any woodworker who does not own this machine. My own drill press dates back several decades, but it still provides good service. (See the photo below.) To make a drill press useful for cabinetmaking work, you have to build a wood table that includes an adjustable fence on which stops can be positioned. The placement of the fence and stops allow you to position parts precisely, which is essential when boring doors for concealed hinges and drilling holes for handles and pulls. I also use my drill press for sanding and certain routing operations.

Bandsaw

A bandsaw sure is a nice tool to have for general woodworking, but it's not a must for building kitchen cabinets. I use my bandsaw mainly for cutting curved door parts, but that is a job you can do with a good jigsaw.

For woodworking applications, a drill press needs to have a shop-made auxiliary table and fence. By adjusting the fence position and setting up stops, you can bore holes exactly where they need to be.

PRO **TIP**

To get a clean cut with a sliding compound-miter saw, remember to pull the saw out, then lower the blade and push it through the stock.

WHAT CAN GO WRONG

The high level of moisture in the average basement can cause steel to rust, and there's plenty of steel in a workshop—from bits and blades to machinery surfaces and hardware. There are several ways to fight rust, even in a damp basement. Running a dehumidifier removes moisture from the air. Coating chisels and sawblades with silicone spray helps them resist rusting. Steel or cast-iron machine surfaces can be protected from rust with a coat of paste wax. Applying buffing wax on the top of a table saw also helps the workpiece slide more smoothly.

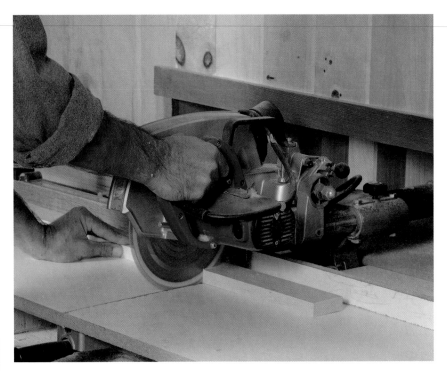

This sliding compound-miter saw is set up in a workstation that includes an extended auxiliary table for supporting long boards and a long fence for keeping stock aligned.

Chopsaw

Although the chopsaw is considered a portable power tool, it's always set up as a stationary machine in a cabinet shop. Woodworkers rely on the chopsaw to make exact cuts in boards and molding. A good chopsaw can be adjusted easily to make cuts at just about any angle and bevel. This work can also be done on a table saw, but a chopsaw does the job faster and with less fuss.

The chopsaw that I use most often is a sliding compound-miter saw, so named because it can slide along a pair of rails and make compound (beveled and angled) cuts. The blade and motor housing plunge (chop) down into the workpiece. (See the photo above.) For ease and accuracy, your chopsaw must be bolted to a solid bench or table, with extensions set up on both sides to support long stock. You'll also need

Made from two layers of melamine-coated particleboard, my router table is large enough to hold two routers. Separate wall-mounted switches control each one. One of my many shop-made fences hangs on the wall.

some way to set up stop blocks so cuts can be repeated exactly.

Router table

A router table doesn't need to be fancy or elaborate. In fact, I keep my own router table nice and simple. (See the bottom photo on the facing page.) I use two layers of ¾-in.-thick melamine-coated particleboard to make a flat, strong, durable, and inexpensive top. I made the top large enough to hold two routers, which makes certain joinery operations (cutting dovetails, for example) go more quickly. Add some legs and a wall-mounted switch to turn the router on and off, and you're nearly done. I like to make my own fences and simply clamp them to the tabletop. Rather than rely on a single fence, I tend to make fences to suit specific functions, building them from hardboard, plywood, or particleboard.

Some woodworkers prefer to use a shaper instead of a router table; in other shops, you'll find both machines hard at work. (See the sidebar at right.) However you do your shaping work, your investment in bits will soon equal or exceed the price of an average router or entry-level shaper.

Portable Power Tools and Accessories

It's great but also perplexing to find such a tremendous selection of portable power tools at home centers and in mail-order catalogs. My advice on buying these tools is to try them out whenever possible. Although you can't operate these tools at a home center, you can test their weight and feel and see how well the controls and adjustments work for you. It's also smart to solicit brand and model preferences from experienced woodworkers.

Shaper vs. Router Table

The traditional argument that professional woodworkers use shapers while amateurs use router tables is long gone. These days, some entry-level shapers sell for less than you'd pay for a router and router table setup.

Shapers are heavy machines; even the smallest ones can weigh 200 lbs. or more. They have interchangeable spindles for ½-in. or ¾-in. cutters, and the typical small-shop shaper has a collet that accepts router bits. A shaper excels at spinning large bits (including router bits) to remove major amounts of material. A shaper can remove in a single pass what would take a router table several passes. However, small bits don't perform well in a shaper because they require a router's top speed (22,000 rpm or so) to deliver smooth cuts. A shaper has a reversible induction motor, which gives you more flexibility when using shaper cutters. A router table has the option of removing the router to use in freehand operations. Given these pros and cons, it's no wonder that many woodworkers eventually come to own a router as well as a shaper. But if you can only buy one tool, make it a router table.

For speed and convenience, team up a cordless drill with quick-change drill-and-drive accessories.

PRO TIP

To make better use of space in a small shop, put your table saw or planer on a mobile base. These bases are available where woodworking machinery is sold.

IN DETAIL

The electric motor that comes with a table saw, bandsaw, or other stationary machine is normally capable of operating on either 115- or 220-volt current. The way the wires are arranged in the motor's junction box determines the operating voltage. A motor runs at slightly better efficiency with 220-volt current, but the difference is negligible. Also, 220-volt wiring requires special circuitry at your service panel and special plugs and receptacles. For these reasons, most small workshops do fine on 115 volts. However, to avoid tripping circuit breakers or blowing fuses, the receptacles that serve power tools in your shop should be on 20-amp circuits. Note that 15-amp circuits should be used for shop lighting only.

Cordless drill/driver

This is the tool you'll be using day in and day out for any cabinetmaking project. You need a drill to bore pocket and pilot holes for screws and to drive screws when assembling cabinet cases, face frames, and bases. Although I have a corded drill, I use cordless versions for all but the most power-hungry assignments, such as using a saw hole cutter when installing cabinets.

There are many good cordless drill/drivers on the market. For cabinetmaking, a 12- or 14-volt model provides more than adequate power. Make sure that your drill/driver kit includes an extra battery so you don't have to stop working when one battery runs out of power. To make the most of this power tool, you'll also need some quick-change bit accessories, as shown in the photo on p. 13. Buy a basic set of "drill-and-drive" bits, including combination countersink/counterbore bits and Phillips-head bits in several lengths. This will set you up well for pocket-hole joinery (see below) and assembly work.

Pocket-hole jigs

Pocket-hole joinery dates back to ancient Egypt. Today, pocket-hole jigs have helped cabinetmakers save time and simplify joinery details without sacrificing quality or strength. Major cabinet manufac-

Fast, strong, and reversible, joinery with pocket screws is very useful in cabinet construction. In the photo above, a pocket-hole jig with a toggle clamp is used to bore a pair of holes in a face-frame rail. In the photo at right above, I clamp a single-hole jig in position to bore holes in a case side. In the photo at right, mating face-frame parts are clamped together while pocket screws are driven.

A biscuit joiner cuts crescent-shaped slots in mating parts so that an oval biscuit can be glued in place, strengthening and aligning the joint.

turers have pocket-hole machines with pneumatic clamps and other sophisticated features. I have a couple of basic pocket-hole jigs that I use for various joints. Made by the Kreg Tool Company® (see Resources on p. 165), these jigs are affordable and very easy to use. They are designed to guide a drill bit so it bores a pilot hole at a shallow angle. (See the photos on the facing page.) The mating part is then clamped against the part with the pocket hole so the joint can be screwed fast with special self-drilling panhead screws.

Biscuit joiner

Also called a plate joiner, this portable slot-cutting machine has become one of the most important tools in my shop. After slots are cut in mating parts, biscuits are glued in the slots to align and strengthen the joint. (See the photos above.) Biscuit joinery is fast and easy. The tool's depth setting is adjustable, enabling you to cut crescent-shaped slots for different-size biscuits. There's also a fence that can be moved up and down or set at different angles, allowing you to cut slots in beveled edges and in stock of varying thicknesses.

The price range for biscuit joiners starts at under $100 and goes up to $600 and more. No matter which model and make you buy, you will find many applications for this tool long after your cabinet project is done.

Random-orbit sander

Versatility is what makes this tool valuable. Depending on the grit of sandpaper used, a random-orbit sander can remove stock aggres-

With a random-orbit sander, you can handle a wide range of sanding tasks. By replacing the standard flat backing pad with a resilient foam pad, you can sand curved surfaces, such as the edges of raised panels.

IN DETAIL

A cordless drill is one of the most frequently used tools in the shop. But there are times when you'll need a corded model. Power-demanding applications like using large forstner bits or hole saws can drain a fully charged battery in less than a minute.

TRADE SECRET

Make sure that you always have a fully charged spare battery when working with cordless power tools. Most batteries will hold a charge longer if you run the battery down completely before recharging it.

+ SAFETY FIRST

Safety in the workshop involves equipment, behavior, and attitude. Here's what you can do to maintain a solid safety record:

- **Protect your eyes and ears.** Have safety goggles and hearing protectors for you and anyone else in the shop.
- **Keep a first-aid kit nearby.** Make sure that it contains a small plastic bag or two, in case you need to transport a severed finger to the hospital. When packed in ice, severed digits can often be reattached successfully.
- **Follow fire-prevention procedures.** Mount a fire extinguisher in an accessible location. Dispose of flammable materials (sawdust and oil-soaked rags) before they accumulate. Remember that an oil-soaked rag can spontaneously combust unless it's kept in an airtight container.
- **Work in a well-lit shop.**
- **Keep your work area clean and uncluttered.**
- **Always unplug power tools before changing blades or bits.**
- **Keep edges sharp.** Whether you're using a chisel, a bit, or a blade, sharp edges tend to be safer because they cut without being forced. Increasing feed pressure raises the risk of injury.
- **Practice on scrap material.** If you haven't tried a woodworking technique or operation before (especially with power tools), take a trial run or two on some scrap material. Make sure you can keep your hands well away from the cutting edges and that the workpiece can stay properly positioned from start to finish. If an operation seems dangerous, it probably is; figure out how to make it safer.
- **Avoid distractions.** Children, dogs, guests, and other distractions can divert your attention at critical moments.

sively or get the wood surface super smooth in preparation for finishing. Keep an ample supply of sanding discs on hand, and stock them in grits ranging from 80 to 220. The Porter Cable® sander that I use has a flat, stiff pad that is good for sanding flat surfaces. To sand contours, such as the curved edge of a raised panel, I switch to a softer pad. (See the photo on the previous page.)

Although you'll be able to do most of your sanding with a random-orbit sander, you can also expect to do some hand sanding, so it's a good idea to maintain a supply of sandpaper sheets in different grits.

Brad nailer

I think of my brad nailer as an extra set of hands that doesn't demand wages. Powered by a small air compressor, this compact nailer drives 18-gauge brads in lengths that range from ½ in. to 1½ in. (See the photo below.) I never use brads as primary fasteners. The tool's value is in tacking parts in place until glue sets or more substantial fasteners can be driven. With a brad nailer, I can hold the part exactly in position with one hand, then tack it in place with the other. That's faster and

An air-powered brad nailer works like a third hand, enabling you to tack parts in place quickly and often eliminating the need for clamps.

easier than trying to keep the part positioned while driving a nail or screw by hand. If you don't have a helper in your shop, you need a brad nailer.

The air compressor that powers a brad nailer is useful for other tasks as well. Put an air nozzle at the end of the air hose, and you can quickly and thoroughly blow sawdust off tools and workbenches. A compressor can power spray-finishing equipment and other pneumatic tools, such as sanders and impact wrenches. A good way to buy a compressor is in a kit, which includes a compressor, an air hose, and a brad nailer. Kit prices start at around $300.

A bevel gauge is often used to transfer an angle directly to the blade of a table saw, allowing you to cut a matching angle.

Other Tools and Equipment

Clamps often play a role in cabinet construction. Pipe clamps are helpful for gluing up panels and other aspects of cabinet construction. And I've come to view my wide-mouth locking clamp as indispensable. This clamp enables me to quickly lock two parts together, screw them fast, and then release the clamp simply by pressing a lever. Layout tools are essential for cabinetmaking. A good tape measure, a combination square, a framing square, and a 4-ft. level are important tools for building and installing cabinets. Also make sure

you have a bevel gauge on hand. (See the photo above.) You'll find it useful for transferring angles from the edge of a board to the table saw.

Don't forget your workbench. You need a flat, solid work surface where parts can be spread out, organized, and assembled. I also use my table saw's outfeed table as a work surface. Finally, remember that this is just the beginning. As you become more experienced, you'll discover more tools and accessories that can help you. You'll also start to invent your own jigs, shop helpers, and shortcuts, such as the T-shaped supports shown in the photo below.

A pair of T-shaped supports comes in handy when you're organizing and assembling parts. Made from ¾-in.-thick plywood, the supports hold the work flat above your workbench, leaving room for clamps underneath.

Understanding

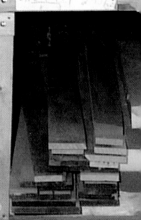

CHAPTER TWO

Wood

1 Composite-Wood Panels, p. 20

2 Solid Wood, p. 24

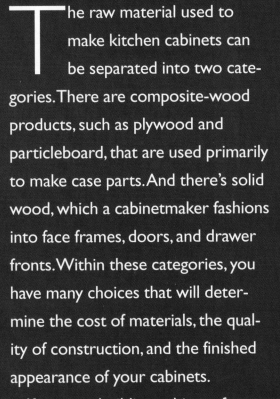

3 Sources for Lumber, p. 27

The raw material used to make kitchen cabinets can be separated into two categories. There are composite-wood products, such as plywood and particleboard, that are used primarily to make case parts. And there's solid wood, which a cabinetmaker fashions into face frames, doors, and drawer fronts. Within these categories, you have many choices that will determine the cost of materials, the quality of construction, and the finished appearance of your cabinets.

If you are building cabinets from scratch, you can expect to spend more than two-thirds of your budget on raw materials. That's why it's important to have a good understanding of what's available, how much it costs, and what strengths and limitations different materials have. So, let's get started.

TRADE SECRET

To learn about cabinetmaking materials, spend some time in showrooms where factory-made cabinetry is on display. Major home centers and kitchen cabinet suppliers display a wide range of cabinets in their showrooms. You can compare the finished appearance of different wood species used on cabinet doors, drawers, and face frames. See what stained wood looks like in comparison to wood finished with clear varnish or lacquer. Compare drawers made with plywood to those made from solid wood. Getting an overall impression of how material choices affect appearance and quality will help you choose the right products for your cabinetry projects.

Plywood, particleboard, and other sheet goods should be stored in flat, well-organized racks. Inspect the edges for damage before buying these materials.

Composite-Wood Panels

Some woodworkers refer to this category of products as "sheet goods," because it consists of plywood, particleboard, and other products that are manufactured in sheets or panels. (See the photo above.) But the term "composite wood" is also accurate, because these materials are made from wood particles, fibers, and veneers that are bound together with various adhesives and resins. The standard size for all types of panels is 4 ft. wide by 8 ft. long.

Plywood

For decades, plywood has been the staple of cabinet shops. Conventional plywood is made from thin wood veneers, or plies, glued together so that the grain direction in each ply runs at a 90-degree angle to the grain direction in adjacent plies. The number of plies in a sheet is always odd. Many ¼-in.-thick plywood panels contain just three plies. A standard sheet of ¾-in. plywood may contain five or seven plies. Regardless of the number of layers, plywood has a cross-laminated construction that makes it the strongest of all composite products; this also explains its excellent nail- and screw-holding characteristics. Cross-laminated construction also makes plywood very stable; it doesn't shrink, cup, or warp like solid wood does. Plywood is lighter than other composite panels because most manufacturers use lightweight woods (such as poplar and alder) for core veneers.

The plywood used for cabinetmaking applications is usually an interior grade made with non-waterproof adhesive. Most cabinetmakers choose plywood with hardwood face veneers. As shown in the photos on the facing page, face veneers are typically much thinner than core veneers. Just about any wood species can be used as a face veneer, but cabinetmakers often choose the same species that will be used for the face frames, doors,

Cross-laminated veneers, or plies, give plywood its strength and stability.

Plywood: An Ancient Material

Egyptian carpenters are credited with the invention of plywood. A coffin from the Saqqara Pyramid, dating back to 2750 B.C.E., was made out of plywood. Fragments from the coffin clearly showed six layers of veneer, glued and doweled, with the grain of each layer running in alternate directions, just as it does in today's plywood.

The mass production of wood veneer began in Europe around 1850, and woodworking shops started turning out plywood panels in the 1890s. In the U.S., the most significant breakthrough in plywood production came during World War II, when waterproof glue was developed to make mahogany plywood for PT boats.

In cabinet grades of plywood, the face veneers are much thinner than the core veneers.

and drawer fronts. Alternatively, it's possible to select a species that can be stained or finished to look like the solid wood used elsewhere in the cabinet. Birch-veneered plywood can look very much like maple, for example, and alder can be stained to resemble cherry.

Plywood's main disadvantage is its high cost. A 4×8 sheet of ¾-in. birch plywood can sell for $50 or more. And unlike other composite panels, standard plywood contains core voids—gaps in the core veneer that occur during the manufacturing process. These voids can sometimes weaken the panel or make joinery difficult when they occur near an edge. Baltic birch plywood is a premium-grade plywood that has 13 plies in a ¾-in.-thick panel, and no core voids are allowed. (See the sidebar on p. 22.)

Other types of plywood. Instead of using standard plywood to make case parts, some cabinetmakers and manufacturers have switched to plywood that has a particleboard or medium-density fiberboard (MDF) core. Plywood made with those core materials (which are described later) is less expensive than standard plywood but

TRADE SECRET

To locate a lumberyard or specialty lumber dealer, look under "Lumber" in the Yellow Pages®. You'll also find sources for cabinetmaking wood in the back of woodworking magazines and on the Internet. Some of these companies specialize in just a few woods, while others stock a wide selection.

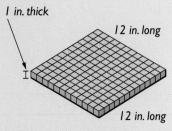

1 in. thick

12 in. long

12 in. long

Each block is 1 in. wide, 1 in. long, 1 in. tall

IN DETAIL

Molding and trim are sold by the lineal foot (lf.). Solid wood boards are usually sold by volume, using a measure called "board feet" (bd. ft.). You can calculate the bd. ft. contained in a piece of solid wood using this formula: nominal thickness (in.) × nominal width (in.) × actual length (in.) divided by 144. For example, a 1×6 board that's 8 ft. long comes to 4 bd. ft.: (1×6×96)/144 = 4.

Alternatives to standard plywood (second sheet from the top) include MDF-core (top), particleboard-core (third from the top), and combined-core (bottom) panels.

looks the same from the outside. (See the photo at left.)

However, there are some disadvantages to consider. First of all, particleboard and MDF don't have the moisture-resistant qualities that standard plywood has. They're much heavier, too. And these materials don't hold screws or nails as well as standard plywood does. To overcome these limitations, manufacturers have developed composite-core plywood, which is made by sandwiching a pair of cross-laminated solid wood plies between core layers of particleboard or MDF. To order that type of plywood, you'll probably need to contact a specialty lumber dealer or commercial plywood supplier.

Baltic Birch Plywood

Some woodworkers consider Baltic birch plywood to be the ultimate composite material, and it's easy to understand why. Standard plywood has thick core plies made from inexpensive wood (poplar, for example) that is relatively soft and weak. Baltic birch plywood is made by gluing together thin birch veneers. The core voids found in standard plywood are not allowed in Baltic birch. These two differences make Baltic birch stronger and more stable than standard plywood.

And thanks to its uniform, void-free construction, Baltic birch produces beautiful machined edges. Although most woodworkers consider Baltic birch to be too heavy and too expensive for case parts, it's an ideal material for drawer boxes.

Because it's manufactured in Europe, Baltic birch comes in metric sizes (see the chart below) and panels measure approximately 5 ft. square. U.S. versions of this plywood are also available— ApplePly®, for example.

Nominal thickness	Actual thickness	Plies
5/32 in.	4mm	3
1/4 in.	5mm	5
15/64 in.	6mm	5
3/8 in.	9mm	7
1/2 in.	12mm	9
19/32 in.	15mm	11
3/4 in.	18mm	13

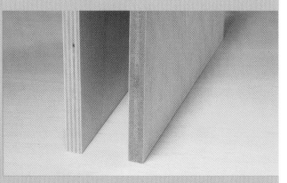

Because more plies are used and there are no core voids, Baltic-birch plywood (shown above) is stronger and more stable than standard hardwood plywood. It's heavier and more expensive, too.

Particleboard

The least expensive sheet material for cabinet cases is particleboard. This product is made from wood waste that is ground up into particles, mixed with a binder, and pressed into panels. Most particleboard has three layers. A core of coarse particles is sandwiched between face layers made from a finer material to provide smooth outer surfaces.

Particleboard is not a strong as plywood. A ¾-in.-thick shelf that spans more than 24 in. will sag under its own weight. Particleboard doesn't grip fasteners as well as plywood, and exposure to moisture will make the material swell and even break apart. To make particleboard more useable for cabinet parts, manufacturers coat it with melamine. Melamine-coated particleboard (MCP) is often used to build European-style frameless cabinets, but it can also be used instead of plywood for cabinet case parts. The melamine coating—actually a layer of melamine-impregnated paper—gives particleboard a smooth, hard, moisture-resistant finish. (See the top photo on p. 24.) It doesn't increase the strength of the material or improve screw-holding ability, though. MCP has more moisture resistance than plain particleboard, but the coating doesn't prevent moisture damage.

Particleboard is used by many large cabinet manufactures because of its low cost.

Grades of Hardwood Plywood

Most hardwood plywood is manufactured according to grading standards established by the American National Standards Institute (ANSI). Hardwood plywood is graded with a letter for the good, or "show," face of the panel and a number for the back of the panel. The best panel grade is A-1. Face grades range from A to E; back grades, from 1 to 4. For ½-in. to ¾-in. thickness, a typical cabinet plywood grade is A-1 or B-2. For ¼-in. plywood, a typical cabinet plywood grade is A-4.

Face Veneer

"A" Grade
- Bookmatched
- Slight mineral streaks and vine marks
- No sound or repaired knots
- Conspicuous burls maximum size: ⅜ in.
- Two ¹⁄₁₆-in. by 6-in. repaired hairline splits allowed

"B" Grade
- May be bookmatched
- Slight mineral streaks
- Vine marks, small repaired knots, conspicuous burls
- Two ⅛-in. by 6-in. repaired hairline splits allowed

"C" Grade
- Not bookmatched
- Mineral streaks and vine marks acceptable
- No limit to pin knots and small burls
- Up to eight sound and repaired knots
- Up to four ³⁄₁₆-in. by 8-in. repaired hairline splits

Back Veneer

"1" Back
- Up to 16 sound tight knots
- No knotholes
- Sound tight burls
- Mineral streaks
- Up to six repaired splits or joints

"2" Back
- Up to 16 sound tight knots
- Repaired knotholes
- Sound tight burls
- Mineral streaks
- Up to six repaired splits or joints

"3" Back
- Larger tight knots
- Larger repaired knots
- Larger repaired splits or joints

"4" Back
- Any species of hardwood
- Unlimited knotholes
- Tight knots, and burls
- Can have open defects

TRADE SECRET

For a smoother run when cutting panels to size on the table saw, make sure the table surface is free of sawdust, then wipe it clean, using window cleaning spray to remove residue or sticky deposits. Buff a light coat of paste wax on the table surface. This will reduce friction, making the panel slide easier. Also make sure the panel is supported adequately on the infeed and outfeed ends of the table saw.

Because of melamine's brittleness, it must be cut with a triple-chip laminate blade to produce a chip-free edge. One final consideration: The melamine surface doesn't bond well with glue, so your cabinet joinery may need to be revised to include dadoes, rabbets, or extra fasteners.

Medium- and high-density fiberboards

Medium-density fiberboard (MDF) and high-density fiberboard (HDF) are made from compressed wood fibers and a resin binder. These brown-colored panels are denser and smoother

Melamine-coated particleboard (MCP) offers an inexpensive way to build cabinet cases with a finish that is already in place.

MDF is heavy and has a fine texture, making it an excellent material for jigs and templates.

than particleboard and have better nail- and screw-holding characteristics. MDF is very stable and consistent but also prone to water damage. When you cut or shape MDF, you get a smooth surface, because the material is uniform and void-free. It's an excellent choice for templates and jigs. MDF can also be covered with wood veneer to give it the appearance of solid wood. Its main disadvantage is its weight. A 1-in.-thick 4×8 ft. sheet can weigh more than 90 pounds.

Solid Wood

Fine cabinetry and solid wood go hand in hand. Solid wood is used to make the most visible parts of a completed cabinet—the doors, drawers, face frame, end panel, and crown molding. The wood you choose for your cabinets will have a major impact on the construction process and the finished appearance.

The selection process involves several factors. First, select the species of wood, and perhaps even a subgroup within that species. At the same time, decide which type of finish treatment you want to use to show off the wood in your cabinets. (See Chapter 10.) At the lumber dealer, examine different grades of wood, balancing the grain and color characteristics against the budget you've established. Just ahead, I'll go over some of the main species of wood used for cabinets and discuss some of the grading rules that are important to know.

Wood species

I divide solid wood into three categories: softwood, hardwood, and exotic wood. Most cabinets are built from domestic hardwoods (the main species are described below). But if you're not on a tight schedule to complete your cabinets (as most professional cabinetmakers are), you can take your time finding just the right wood to use. Some woodworkers like the look of antique or weathered wood. Other people—log-home owners, for example—want their cabinets made from the same wood that forms the walls of the house. You can be sure that the time you spend selecting just the right boards will be well spent.

Maple. Although light in color, maple shows variations in tone. Northern hard maple is the lightest in color and most uniform in texture. It's also the hardest of the maples—it's difficult to work with hand tools and dense enough that shaping an edge requires numerous shallow cuts at progressively deeper settings. Soft maple is generally less expensive, easier to work with, and more varied in color. Figured maple is prized by many cabinetmakers and furniture collectors. Common types of figured maple include tiger maple (which has iridescent stripes that run across the grain) and bird's-eye maple (which has small, randomly spaced, eyelike defects). Because figured wood is very expensive and requires extra skill to cut and smooth, its use on cabinetry commands astronomical prices.

Maple has a subtle grain and light natural color that shouldn't be obscured with dark stain or finishes. Instead, a very light tint gives the wood a light golden "antique maple" appearance.

Oak. For years, oak was the most popular wood for kitchen cabinets. It has always been readily available and nice to work with. If you are looking for attractive grain patterns and a solid, traditional look, oak is your material. Northern red oak is more common and less expensive than white oak.

Because oak has a coarse grain, it does not take finish as smoothly as other woods. Semi-paste wood fillers are sometimes applied to fill oak's open pores and create a smoother surface for finishing.

Cherry. Many woodworkers name cherry as their favorite wood. It works very well with hand tools and machining is no problem. To avoid dark

Maple is naturally light in tone, but darker grains can also be found. This strong, tight-grained wood has excellent durability.

burn marks on cut or machined edges, be sure to keep your tools sharp and your machines aligned. Cherry sapwood is light in color; the heartwood of freshly cut or planed cherry is light orange/red in color. With exposure to light, this wood turns a beautiful burgundy color. Applying cherry stain to other woods, such as maple, also produces this color, but it looks dull compared to the real thing. If you want instant dark cherry cabinets, I recommend using red alder and staining it. Alder has the same grain texture as cherry, but it is much less expensive.

Cherry's only drawback is its high cost. Depending on where you live, cherry can be twice as expensive as maple or oak. An average

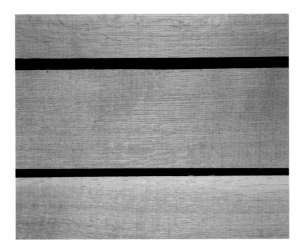

Oak is one of the most affordable hardwoods, but it can be challenging to finish because of its coarse grain.

25

TRADE SECRET

If you do your woodworking in a basement shop or another area where humidity tends to be high, it may be necessary to reduce the amount of moisture in the air. Signs of excess humidity include rust on metal surfaces, the presence of mold, warping of straight boards stored in your shop, and excessive wood shrinkage when projects are finished and moved out of your shop.

There are two proven ways to reduce humidity problems in a workshop. First, make sure you store your wood properly. (See the main text and the top photo on p. 29.) Second, run a dehumidifier in your shop. Heavy-duty models are designed to run continuously, emptying water into a floor drain. Other models are designed to shut off when a reservoir is filled. A major appliance dealer should be able to help you find a model that meets your needs.

kitchen uses approximately 500 board ft. of lumber. The difference between cherry and oak just for the solid wood may be more than $1,000.

Hickory. In the last several years, more and more hickory cabinets have made their way into showrooms. Some of the prettiest cabinets I build are made from hickory. This wood has an open grain like that of oak, but with much more color variation. A wall of hickory doors and drawer fronts is a celebration of wood's unique character.

However, you'll find this wood quite difficult to work with. Many boards have an irregular grain, which means you can expect more tearout than with other species. And hickory expands and contracts more than other woods do in response to changes in humidity. If your cabinetry will be exposed to high humidity and very dry conditions over the course of a year, you may have problems with excessive swelling and shrinkage. I recommend thoroughly prefinishing hickory parts (such as raised panels) before assembly.

Although hickory costs around the same as maple, I always order about 30% extra because there will be more waste material when cutting and machining this wood. If you are willing to put

Hickory has a coarse grain like that of oak, but there's more color variation and the grain patterns are often wild.

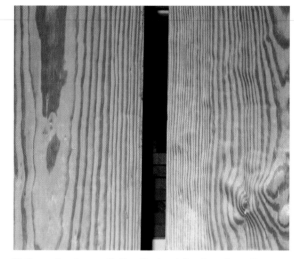

Yellow pine has a distinctively striped grain pattern.

up with hickory's finicky nature, you'll be rewarded with a spectacular kitchen.

Other woods. Although hardwoods are more popular than softwoods for kitchen cabinetry, you can build a beautiful set of cabinets from yellow or white pine, two softwoods that are affordable and easy to work with. Yellow pine is primarily grown in the southeastern U.S. and typically displays a distinct contrast between the early wood and the late wood that make up its grain pattern. (See the photo above.) White pine has a less dramatic grain pattern, with color that varies from off-white to light brown.

Lumber milled from locally harvested trees is also worth considering. And if you want to go to the opposite extreme, it's possible to make cabinets from mahogany, teak, and other exotic woods that come from faraway forests. But before you buy a load of unfamiliar wood, make sure you talk with a few experienced woodworkers about the species that interest you. You need to know how a wood cuts and machines, how dimensionally stable it is, which glue works best with it, and which finishes are recommended. Keep in mind that it takes several hundred board feet of solid wood for the average kitchen. You don't want to invest time and money in a material with unknown characteristics.

Grades of solid wood

There are eight grades of hardwood currently in use, but woodworkers usually stick with the top four grades so they can work with high-quality lumber. The important thing to know about grading is that it's based on the percentage of clear, defect-free area found on the faces of a board.

- **FAS.** Short for "First and Seconds," FAS is the highest hardwood grade. An FAS board must be at least 8 in. wide. Expect to pay a premium price.
- **FAS 1-Face.** Abbreviated as "F1F," this Select board is at least 6 in. wide.
- **Select.** The minimum board width for Select wood is 3 in. The poor or bad side of a Select board is graded as No. 1 Common (see below), while the good side is graded as FAS.
- **No. 1 Common.** This grade, often referred to as "Common" or "No. 1," is frequently used for furniture. You can expect to cut out some defects in these boards, which must be at least 3 in. wide.
- **No. 2 Common.** Also a popular furniture grade because of its affordability, No. 2 Common has slightly more defects than No. 1; the minimum width is 3 in.

Sources for Lumber

There are many sources for good-quality lumber. Major home centers stock popular species, including oak, pine, and maple. The boards are kiln-dried and planed to 4/4 (¾-in.) thickness—just what you need for making face frames, doors, and drawer fronts. You're free to sort through the selection of boards and pick out what you need.

Despite the convenience of major home centers, most small woodshops purchase their lumber from distribution yards. These lumber dealers sell in quantities as small as 100 board ft. and as large as a truckload. The selection of species and grades varies depending on the yard. Getting boards

thicker than ¾ in. is no problem at a lumber dealer, and most large yards deliver within their local area. Some yards also offer services such as planing and ripping for a fee.

Depending on your location, it may be possible to go directly to a sawmill rather than a lumber

Lumber Drying Problems

The solid wood used for cabinetmaking must be dry—a moisture content of 8% to 12% works best for most woodworkers. Whether wood is allowed to dry out in the open air or loaded into a kiln to speed the drying process, there are several problems that can occur. Here's a brief overview.

- **Case hardening.** This occurs when the outside of the board has a lower moisture content than the inside. Although no visible problems are evident, the moisture differential creates tension within the board that is released when the board is cut. As shown in the photo below, the kerf made by the blade may close up, pinching the blade and possibly causing kickback. Don't try to cut a case-hardened board. If the board is reasonably flat, run it through a thickness planer to remove the drier wood from both faces so the moisture content can equalize.
- **Honeycomb.** Deep checks, some of which may be hidden beneath a sound wood surface, are referred to as honeycomb. This condition is also caused by major moisture differences within a board, making wood fibers pull apart and creating voids. Honeycomb is more common in thick stock than in the ¾-in.-thick boards used to build kitchen cabinets. If you encounter this defect, it's best to discard the board.
- **Ring shake.** Ring shake or ring failure occurred in the living tree. This problem is hard to detect on green lumber, when it is measured and graded. The kiln drying will separate the fibers or rings and the shake sometimes becomes clearly visible and sometimes not. When the kiln-dried lumber is not reinspected, shaky boards are left in a lumber stack and shipped to the customer. Ring shake boards are extremely dangerous to machines, especially rotary cutters such as shapers, routers, and lathes.

Cutting a case-hardened board can be dangerous because the kerf often pinches shut.

A well-stocked lumber-yard carries at least several species of wood, and you can select boards in different dimensions.

IN DETAIL

As a solid wood board dries, it develops drying stress caused by opposing forces of compression and tension.

Wood begins to dry from the outside in (A). If the core of a board remains saturated as the outer shell begins to dry and shrink, the shell will develop surface checks. Depending on the moisture gradient between the shell and the core, checking can be limited to the surface or extend deep into the wood. When the shell dries out and stabilizes while the core is still losing moisture, internal cracks (honeycomb) can develop (B). A board that dries out evenly and gradually will continue to expand and contract as moisture is absorbed and lost (C).

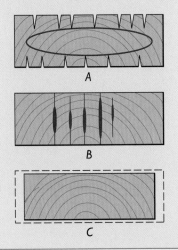

A

B

C

dealer. In parts of the country where trees are harvested for lumber, you can usually find independently owned sawmills that produce a steady supply of native lumber. Some sawyers have portable sawmills and can go to your property and transform logs into lumber.

When you deal directly with a sawmill, you'll get great prices and the opportunity to pick out some exceptional boards. But there are some disadvantages, too. Unless the sawmill has a kiln, its lumber will be green or air-dried. Purchase a lumber moisture meter so you can test the moisture content of the boards you'd like to buy. (See the photo below.) Kiln-dried cabinet lumber normally has a moisture

A moisture meter can help you avoid problems with wood shrinkage or swelling after your cabinets have been built and installed.

content in the 8% to 12% range. If your wood tests out wetter, it will need to lose more moisture by air- or kiln-drying. For details on drying problems that can affect the workability of lumber, see the sidebar on p. 27.

Finally, be aware that a sawmill probably won't sort lumber by grade. Instead, roughsawn boards are simply stacked in piles as they come off the saw. Be prepared to examine every board you buy if you want to avoid defects that can make stock unusable. It's also smart to examine the board's end grain. The orientation of the grain will tell you where the board was cut in the log. (See the left drawing on the facing page.) Vertical growth ring boards are more dimensionally stable than curved end grain boards.

Stickering lumber

No matter where you get your lumber, it's a major investment that you'll want to protect. Always store solid wood out of the weather and up off the ground or floor. It's good practice to "sticker" your boards, using thin strips of scrap wood to separate each layer. (See the photo on the facing page.) Make sure the wood stickers are a uniform thickness, and place them at right angles to the stacked boards every 12 in. or so. This time-tested storage technique keeps boards flat and helps prevent warping.

"Stickering" lumber with thin strips of wood that separate each layer of boards is a good way to maintain flatness and prevent warping.

Grain Orientation and Wood Movement

It's normal for wood to shrink as it dries. Even after it has dried, a board expands and contracts in response to changes in humidity. The orientation of the growth rings in the end of a board can give you a good idea of how the wood will move.

Curving endgrain means that the board will be subject to both radial and tangential shrinkage. Cupping is very likely.

Boards with slanting end grain tend to move diagonally, skewing corners out of square.

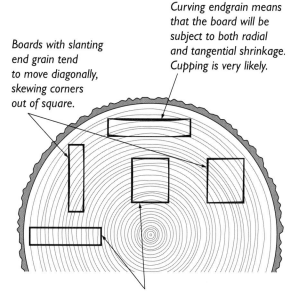

Vertical end grain boards are not likely to cup and are more dimensionally stable than other boards.

Common Lumber Defects

- **Twist** (also called wind). This can occur when the grain direction changes in a board. Short, straight pieces can usually be cut from a board that is not substantially twisted.

- **Cup.** A narrow board (less than 6 in. wide) that's slightly cupped can be planed flat. Otherwise, the best strategy is to rip a cupped board in half and flatten both halves separately.

- **Crook.** This often indicates the presence of reaction wood that will remain unstable; this defect should be avoided.

- **End splits.** Uneven drying often causes end splitting. Examine splits closely to see whether any extend toward the center of the board. If they do, it's better to rip the board along the split line and reglue it or use the pieces separately.

- **Surface checks.** Uneven drying can cause surface checking, so there could be a problem with case hardening or moisture content.

- **Wave.** An entire load of lumber can be wavy if the boards were stacked improperly. Straightening a wavy board takes plenty of planing and isn't usually worth the time or effort.

- **Knots and knotholes.** If you can cut around these defects to make use of clear wood, it's sometimes worth buying knotty stock because of its reduced price.

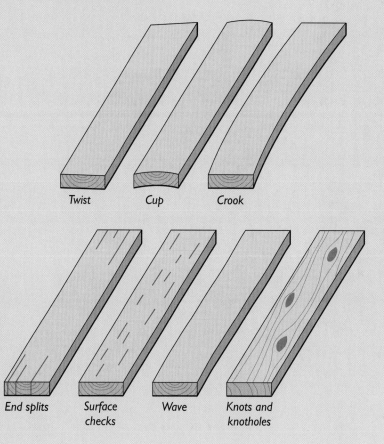

Twist   Cup   Crook

End splits   Surface checks   Wave   Knots and knotholes

Design

CHAPTER THREE

1 Design Ideas, p. 32

2 Making Drawings, p. 32

3 Doors and Drawers, p. 37

4 Designing Custom Cabinets, p. 39

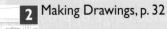

The best reason to build your own kitchen cabinets is that you can get exactly the design and appearance you want. Where cabinet manufacturers are restricted by standard sizes, details, and finishing options, you can customize your cabinets to fit your space, suit your needs, and express your creativity.

There are many decisions to be made when designing a kitchen. In most cases, you won't just be thinking about the cabinets. There will probably be new appliances to consider, as well as lighting schemes, electrical requirements, new flooring, and perhaps even an expanded floor plan. Take your time in evaluating all these design factors, and get help from experts as you need it. Your custom cabinetry deserves an overall kitchen design that's first-rate.

SAFETY FIRST

Include a fire extinguisher in your kitchen design. Most home fires start in the kitchen. Having a fire extinguisher in an accessible spot can save lives and prevent property damage. Buy an extinguisher designated for kitchen use; it's designed to work safely and effectively on flammable liquids and electrical fires. Many models are priced at under $25.

Many combinations of doors and drawers are possible on base cabinets. Deep drawers provide convenient storage for large items, such as pots and pans.

Decide whether you want your doors and drawer fronts to be inset, partial overlay (also known as lipped doors and drawers), or full overlay. (See the drawing below.) I prefer the full-overlay style because it gives a bank of cabinets a pleasing, sleek appearance. The inset treatment is found on more traditional cabinets, while partial-overlay construction is reminiscent of kitchens built in the 1950s.

Now you need to select the style of your doors and which wood species you want to use. Keep in mind that the topmost, or "show," veneer on your cabinet cases should be the same species of wood that you use on the face frames, doors, and drawer fronts.

The traditional cabinet door is a frame-and-panel design that contains one or more raised panels. As you'll see in Chapter 5, there are varia-

Door and Drawer Front Styles

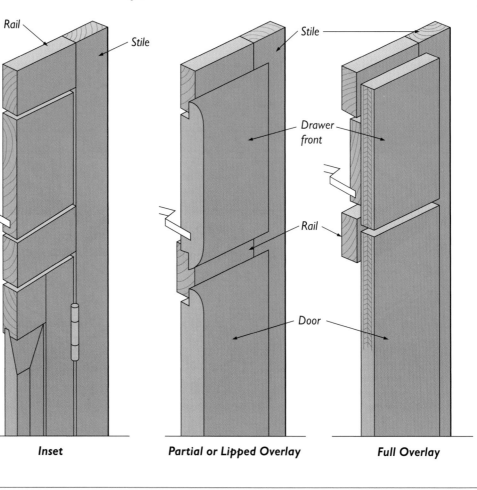

Inset   **Partial or Lipped Overlay**   **Full Overlay**

tions of this door style based on the dimensions of the door parts and the router bits used to shape them. I also build frame-and-panel assemblies to use for the fronts of large drawers. Other door and drawer front designs are also possible, of course. (See the photo at right.) As you'll see later on in this book, if you can build a standard frame-and-panel door, you can learn how to build curved-top and glass-paneled doors as well.

Designing Custom Cabinets

Once you've completed the overall layout of your cabinets, it's time to add all the custom touches that will make this project special. Some refinements will improve the appearance of your cabinets, while others will make the completed kitchen more convenient. This extra effort is what makes a custom kitchen so much better than one with factory-made cabinets. Here are a few ideas to get you started.

Lazy Susans. Plan to install these spinning shelves in base and corner wall cabinets to make these storage spaces more useful.

Pull-out garbage can. You can install this user-friendly feature by mounting a door on an upside-down drawer. For more details, see Chapter 12.

Doors and drawer fronts are the star performers in any kitchen. Learning how to build these parts in different styles can greatly expand your options for custom cabinetry.

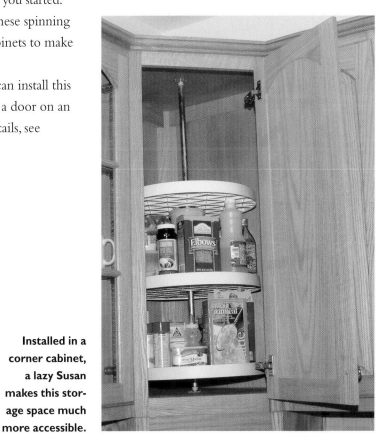

Installed in a corner cabinet, a lazy Susan makes this storage space much more accessible.

PRO TIP

Take the time to make drawings as detailed as possible and remember to study them in every step of building the cabinets.

WHAT CAN GO WRONG

To make the cabinet boxes manageable, I do not recommend a width over 96 in. Even these units can get too heavy if they have mounted, roller-bearing, full-extension drawer slides. If these cabinet units contain many drawers it might be better to make two smaller units instead of one large one. For a one-unit look, lay out the two units with a 1-in. stile on the adjoining face frame.

A pantry cabinet provides a tremendous amount of storage for canned goods and other small items. This one is fitted with pullout drawers.

A pullout garbage can adds convenience. You may want to consider including more than one waste bin or making space for separate recycling bins.

Custom-built pantry cabinets. A full-height pantry cabinet provides a tremendous amount of extra storage space and can also show off some beautiful frame-and-panel joinery. You can customize the interior of the cabinet to hold food items, including canned goods and cereal, or make the space into a storage closet for an upright vacuum and cleaning supplies.

Display shelves. If space allows, consider including some open display shelving in your cabinetry design. Even a couple of small shelves around a window will provide space for small plants or treasured objects.

Curved-top and glass-paneled doors. Once you master the techniques for building standard frame-and-panel doors, you'll be able to step up to a new level of craftsmanship and add these distinctive doors to your repertoire.

Custom storage for special items. Add some custom-built partitions to a base cabinet, and you'll have a great place to store trays and baking sheets. And instead of relying on store-bought plastic trays for silverware and other small items, you can build your own drawer dividers from wood.

Solid wood end panels. A factory-made cabinet has nothing more than a plywood side to show off at the end of a run of cabinets. You can build beautiful frame-and-panel assemblies for end cabinets, using the same tools and techniques that apply to cabinet doors. Another embellishment you can add is an angled end panel—a nice alternative to the square corner found on factory-made cabinets.

As I mentioned earlier, these are just a few of the special touches you can incorporate into your cabinets to make them special. You'll find other design ideas throughout this book. And with every project you take on, you'll discover new ways to define your own brand of custom cabinetry.

Open shelves can be incorporated into a cabinet design to create special spaces for plants or curios.

At the end of a run of cabinets, you can build a beautiful solid wood end panel. An angled corner board with fluting and rosette details contributes to the custom-built appearance.

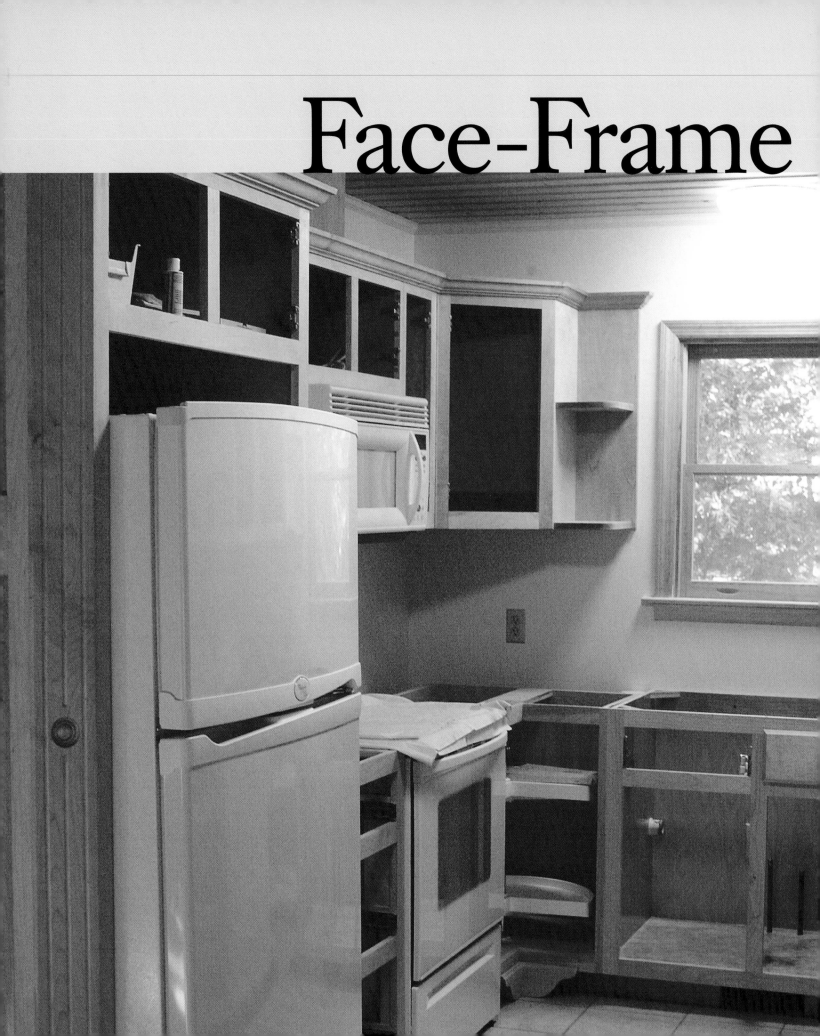

CHAPTER FOUR

Construction

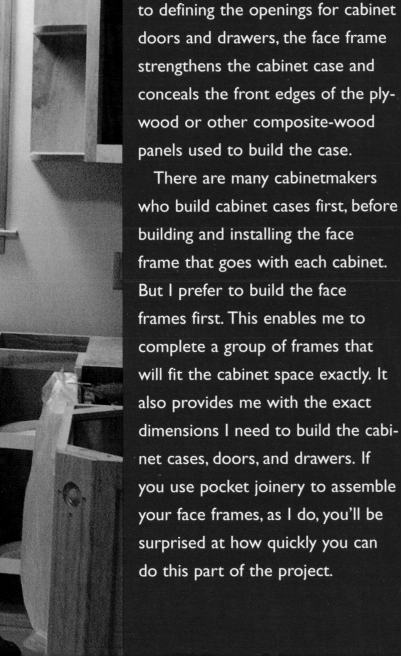

Traditionally, the front of a cabinet is covered by a rectangular frame called a face frame. Vertical members, called stiles, are joined to horizontal rails to form the face frame. In addition to defining the openings for cabinet doors and drawers, the face frame strengthens the cabinet case and conceals the front edges of the plywood or other composite-wood panels used to build the case.

There are many cabinetmakers who build cabinet cases first, before building and installing the face frame that goes with each cabinet. But I prefer to build the face frames first. This enables me to complete a group of frames that will fit the cabinet space exactly. It also provides me with the exact dimensions I need to build the cabinet cases, doors, and drawers. If you use pocket joinery to assemble your face frames, as I do, you'll be surprised at how quickly you can do this part of the project.

1 Dimensioning Face Frames, p. 44

2 Assembling Face Frames, p. 47

TRADE SECRET

Cut your longest face-frame members first, using the straightest boards in your wood supply. Set aside boards that are twisted or bowed. When it's time to cut the shorter stiles and rails on your cutlist, you'll probably be able to get a good number of parts from the less desirable boards.

IN DETAIL

It's usually best for the face frame to be made from the same wood species as the face, or "show," veneer on the plywood used to make the cabinet cases. However, there are instances when this may not be necessary. If you plan to paint your cabinets, for example, birch-veneered plywood and a poplar face frame would be a workable combination. It's also possible to use stain or dye to make one wood species look like another. A face veneer of alder or birch can be stained to resemble a solid cherry face frame.

Dimensioning Face Frames

Before you begin building your face frames, it's good to know how they will be installed when the base and wall cabinets are built. (See Chapters 8 and 9.) As shown in the photo below, the bottom rail of a face frame must align properly with the bottom of the cabinet. Whether it's on a base or a wall cabinet, the inside of the case bottom should be flush with the top edge of the face frame's bottom rail. When attaching the face frame, I use biscuit joints to ensure this alignment. At each side of the cabinet, the face frame extends ¼ in. beyond the outside face of the side. I fasten the face-frame stiles to the cabinet sides with pocket screws. (See the photo at right.) The face frame's top rail can also be pocket-screwed to the top of the case.

Exact measurements are important

On most of the cabinets that I build, the face-frame members are ¾ in. thick and 2 in. wide. Where two face frames will be joined together, I

With pocket screws, secure the face-frame stiles to the case sides. Pocket holes will be hidden when the adjacent cabinet is installed.

The cabinet's inside bottom surface must be flush with the top edge of the face frame's bottom rail. Biscuit joints maintain this alignment when the face frame is installed.

usually make the adjoining stiles just 1 in. wide. This maintains a uniform distance between the doors in adjacent cabinets.

When designing a face frame, another factor to consider is the width of the top rail on wall and pantry cabinets. If you want to finish the wall cabinets with crown molding, it may be necessary to install a wider top rail on them. Choose the molding that you plan to install, then see how wide the top rail needs to be. You can vary the width of stiles or rails if you want to create a different look. Wide frame members let the face frame show more substantially between doors and drawer fronts, giving the finished cabinets an older, more antique look.

Although each cabinet has its own face frame, a number of frames are joined together to form a single assembly when a wall of cabinets is installed. (See the drawing on the facing page.) Any small dimensioning errors will be multiplied when a number of face frames are joined together. For example, if the stiles are cut just

Designing a Face Frame Assembly

To generate the cutlist for cabinet face frames, do an elevation drawing to scale.

• *The standard stile length for base cabinets is 31¾ in.*

• *Rail lengths vary with the cabinet's width.*

• *Stiles that will be joined together when the cabinets are installed can be half the standard width.*

• *A wider top rail provides extra room for installing a crown molding.*

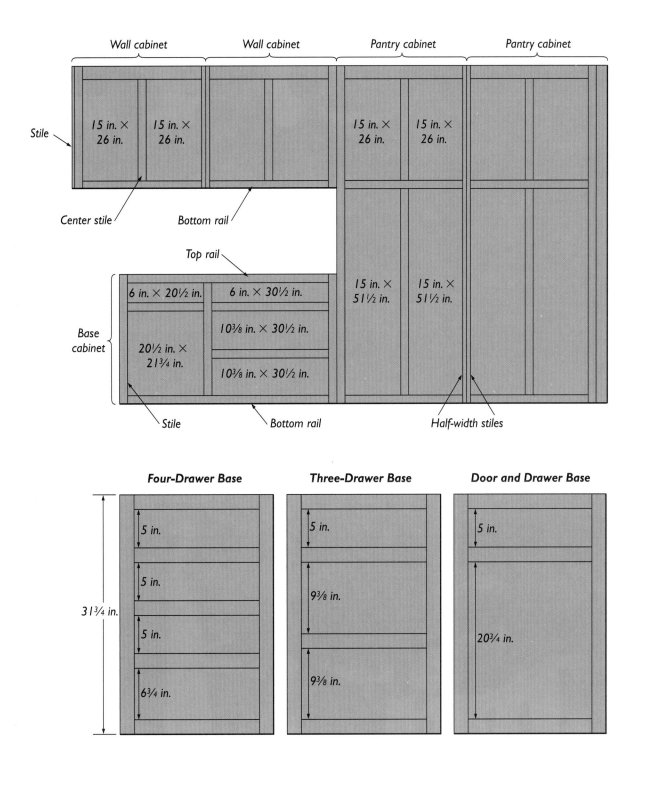

Wall cabinet · Wall cabinet · Pantry cabinet · Pantry cabinet

Stile

15 in. × 26 in. · 15 in. × 26 in. · 15 in. × 26 in. · 15 in. × 26 in.

Center stile · Bottom rail

Top rail

6 in. × 20½ in. · 6 in. × 30½ in.

15 in. × 51½ in. · 15 in. × 51½ in.

10⅜ in. × 30½ in.

Base cabinet

20½ in. × 21¾ in.

10⅜ in. × 30½ in.

Stile · Bottom rail · Half-width stiles

Four-Drawer Base · ***Three-Drawer Base*** · ***Door and Drawer Base***

5 in. · 5 in. · 5 in.

5 in. · 9⅜ in.

31¾ in.

5 in. · 9⅜ in. · 20¾ in.

6¾ in.

Push stick
Workpiece

Cut a ¼-in.-deep notch to fit over the back edge of the workpiece.

IN DETAIL

When ripping narrow face-frame members on a table saw, use a push stick to keep your hand well above the blade. Plastic push sticks are available from mail-order sources and wherever woodworking tools are sold. But it's easy to make your own push stick from some scrap wood.

WHAT CAN GO WRONG

Before cutting any face-frame material to length, make sure you check the 90-degree cut on your chopsaw. You can do this by making test cuts in scrap material, then checking them with a square. If necessary, follow the manufacturer's instructions for adjusting the saw to make perfectly square cuts.

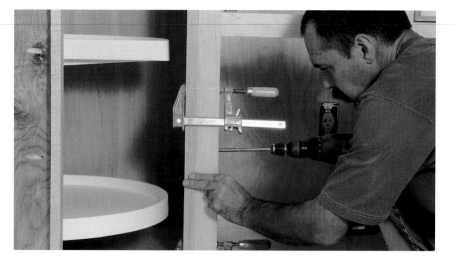

When cabinets are installed, face frames of adjacent cabinets are screwed together.

¹⁄₃₂ in. too wide or too narrow, the completed face-frame assembly could easily be off by more than ¼ in.

Detailed shop drawings will take the confusion out of face-frame measurements. Whether you draw up your face frames on graph paper or use a basic CAD program, a simple front elevation view will give you all the information you need. (See the drawing on p. 45.) If you are joining frame members with pocket screws, dowels, or biscuits, they will simply butt against each other, so it's easy to calculate the lengths of their stiles and rails. If you are assembling frames with traditional mortise-and-tenon joints (see p. 50), you'll have to size the rails and interior stiles to include tenon lengths.

Cutting stiles and rails

Prepare all your face-frame stock at once. Although not essential for building face frames, a jointer and thickness planer are very useful. (See Chapter 1.) There's no guarantee that the boards you buy from the lumberyard will have perfectly straight edges. By running one edge of a board through the jointer, you'll get a straight edge to run against the table saw's rip fence. With just a light pass or two through a thickness planer, you can remove any rough areas on face-frame stock and plane every piece to a uniform thickness. I also use a thickness planer to plane face-frame members to a uniform width. As shown in the photo below, this is done by running pieces on edge through the planer. In planning for this step,

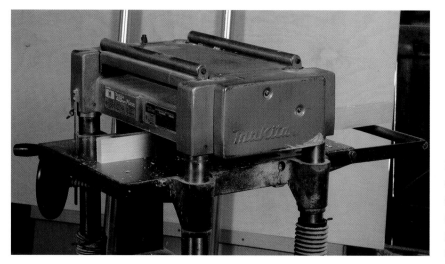

Run face-frame stock on its edge through the planer to remove saw marks and to get all pieces to a uniform width.

A chopsaw equipped with a fine-cutting blade is just what you need to cut face-frame parts to their finished lengths.

I rip the stock slightly wider (between 1/16 in. and 1/8 in.) than its finished width. Plane each edge at least once to get the exact width you need. This strategy has the added benefit of eliminating any saw marks on the edges of your stock.

The next step is to cut the pieces to length with a chopsaw. (See the photo above.) When two or more pieces have to be cut to the same length, set up a stop block to make sure you'll have exact duplicates.

As each piece of a frame is cut, select the best-looking face as the "show" side and label the back so you know where it belongs in the frame. Keep each face frame's stiles and rails grouped together to avoid mixing up the parts.

Assembling Face Frames

The average kitchen has 15 or 20 face frames, with six to eight joints in each frame. It's important to use a joinery method that is fast, accurate, and strong. I prefer pocket–hole joinery to other methods, such as dowels and biscuits. The expense of a pocket hole–drilling jig will easily be repaid in the time you save assembling face frames. And as you'll see elsewhere in this book, pocket holes are very useful for other joinery work, too. Only one piece needs to be drilled when joining two

parts with pocket holes. No glue is required, and frame members can be removed, even after the face frame has been secured to the cabinet box. This makes it possible to replace a damaged frame member or recut a stile or rail to achieve a better fit.

There are different pocket hole–drilling jigs available. The jig I use for face frames includes a clamp that secures the workpiece in exactly the

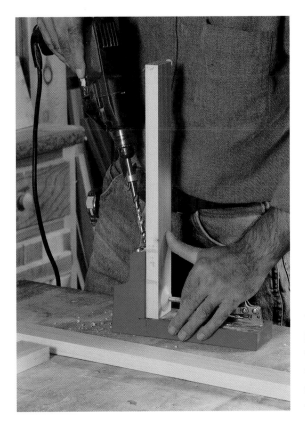

The pocket-hole drilling tool I use has a built-in clamp that holds the workpiece securely. I use a collar-type stop on the drill bit to make sure each hole is bored to exactly the right depth.

PRO TIP

When you fasten a narrow stile or rail with only one pocket screw, keep the piece from turning. Drive a small finishing nail from the side or back of the joint.

The low angle of the pocket holes means that you must drive screws with a long bit that has a square driver tip.

IN DETAIL

Make sure you use special pocket-hole screws when assembling frames with pocket-hole joinery. This type of screw has a flat head and an auger point. It bores its own pilot hole in wood, too. Standard screw lengths are 1¼ in. and 1½ in. At least half the screw's length should extend into the stile or bottom piece. For pocket-hole joinery in hardwood, such as oak and maple, fine-thread screws work best. For softwoods, use screws with coarse threads. The low angle of a pocket hole means that you need to drive screws with a long bit. Most face-frame screws require a square drive bit.

Face-Frame Assembly

"Show" Face

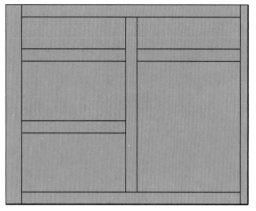

Assembly Face

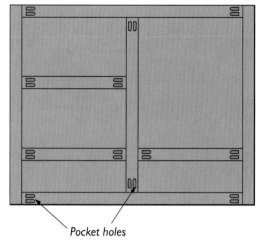

Pocket holes

right position for drilling a pair of angled holes. (See the bottom photo on p. 47.) Along with the drilling jig, I use a special drill bit sized to fit the jig's guide bushings. The process leaves me with two elliptical holes in the workpiece that locate screws below the surface of the wood.

To assemble a single face frame, start by placing all the pieces in their assembled positions on a flat work surface. The "show" face of each stile and rail should face down. As shown in the drawing above, you'll be looking at a mirror image of the frame in its installed orientation.

Once all the holes are drilled, assemble the outermost stiles and rails first—the longest pieces that define the frame's perimeter. Secure each joint with a locking VISE-GRIP® clamp. Then drive the two installation screws. (See the photo below.) The inner stiles and rails come next; these pieces divide a large frame into smaller openings for drawers and doors. To align the inside members, cut spacing strips from scrap wood and place them between the outer frame and the member to be installed. (See the left photo on the facing page.)

The fastest and easiest way to assemble face-frame members is with pocket-hole screws.

Used in pairs, spacer strips can be cut from scrap wood and temporarily placed inside the face frame to ensure the exact alignment of the inner face-frame members.

After assembling a face frame, check it for square by comparing diagonal measurements. A skewed frame assembled with pocket screws can be taken apart and reassembled correctly.

After assembly, check each face frame for square by comparing diagonal measurements. (See the right photo above.) If the two diagonal measurements aren't equal, the frame isn't square. Fortunately, this doesn't spell disaster if you've assembled your frame with pocket screws. Identify where the misaligned or improperly sized piece is, remove it, and reassemble the frame to get it right. Once the frames are completely assembled, set them aside until it's time to install them on the base and wall cabinets. (See Chapters 7 and 8.) It's best to store face frames on a flat surface, out of harm's way, until you attach them to their cases.

Angled face frames for corner cabinets

A corner base cabinet requires a face frame with top and bottom rails that butt together at a 90-degree angle. This cabinet is designed to hold a

Corner Base Cabinet with Face Frame

The corner base cabinet has a right-angled opening that measures 10 in. wide on each side. One pair of rails is 10 in. long; the other is 10¾ in. long.

PRO TIP

Don't glue face-frame joints that are assembled with pocket screws. The glue holds poorly in the end grain of joining pieces, and it can squeeze from the joint.

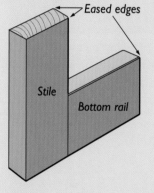

Eased edges

Stile

Bottom rail

TRADE SECRET

After a face frame has been completed, you'll want the frame's outside corners to stay sharp and square. But it's smart to soften the inside corners of the frame—the areas that hands and arms will brush against once the cabinet has been installed and is put to use. You can smooth and just slightly round over these sharp edges with 220-grit sandpaper. But don't give this treatment to the inside bottom corner of the bottom rail, which needs to fit flush against the bottom of the cabinet.

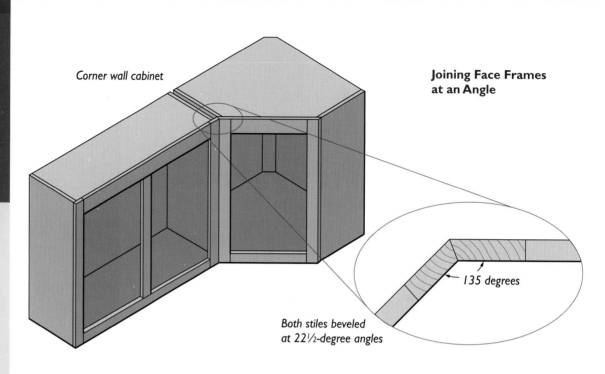

Corner wall cabinet

Joining Face Frames
at an Angle

135 degrees

Both stiles beveled
at 22½-degree angles

kidney-shaped lazy Susan, and the finished opening measures 10 in. across on each side. (See the drawing on p. 49.) The rails for one side of the opening are 10 in. long; the joining rails are 10¾ in. long. The stiles for a corner base cabinet are the same length as those for other base cabinets but you may want to reduce the stile width, because they will join the stiles in neighboring base cabinets. I like to cut and assemble these right-angled face frames along with all the other face frames.

The face frame that goes on a corner wall cabinet is also a little different. As shown in the drawing on p. 45, this face frame joins the frame of a standard wall cabinet to form a 45-degree angle. The edges of the joining stiles need to be beveled at a 22½-degree angle. To make sure you maintain the 2-in. width of each beveled stile, first cut the 22½-degree angle on wider stile stock. Then adjust the rip fence on your table saw so the smaller face of the beveled stile will measure 2 in. wide.

Different ways to join face frames

Even though I am a great fan of pocket-hole joinery, there are other joinery methods that can be used to assemble face frames. Depending on the tools you have available, the time you have to spend, and your joinery preferences, there are three options to consider.

Mortise-and-tenon joints. These joints are strong and traditional, so some dedicated woodworkers still prefer them. Mortises can be cut using a hollow-chisel mortising bit on a drill press or mortising machine. It's also possible to mill mortises using a plunge router equipped with an upcut spiral bit. Tenons can be cut on a table saw or router table.

Dowels. Dowels offer a very economical way to join face frames, and a face-frame joint assembled with a pair of dowels will have more than adequate strength. But don't do dowel joinery unless you have a doweling jig that you can use

Mortise-and-tenon joinery is traditional and time-consuming.

Dowels are inexpensive; a doweling jig is necessary to align holes.

quickly and precisely. The joints must be clamped until the glue sets, and no adjustments are possible.

Biscuits. If I could not use pocket-hole screws to assemble face frames, my second choice would be plate joinery, also called biscuit joinery. These football-shaped wafers fit into slots cut with a biscuit-joiner machine. The main concern with this joinery method is the size of the biscuit. The smallest biscuit—a #0—measures about 2 in. long. If you have 2-in.-wide stock, you are in good shape. But if some members of the face frame are narrower, the slots and biscuits will show outside the joint, so some trimming and filling will be necessary.

No matter which joinery method you use to assemble face frames, you may want to consider building cabinets with beaded frames. This traditional embellishment looks great with inset cabinet doors and drawers. It's also used on bookcases and other built-ins.

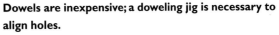

Biscuit joinery is fast and easy, but the size of the biscuit can exceed the width of face-frame members.

BEADED FACE FRAMES

Inset drawers go well with the beaded face frame's on this base cabinet.

Beaded face frames are frequently found on cabinets with inset doors and drawers. A beaded face frame can also be used on cabinetry without doors and drawers—bookcases and cupboards, for example. The bead, or rounded edge, extends around the inside of the frame, with miter joints at the corners. This traditional face-frame treatment is not as difficult to build as you might think. Instead of cutting the bead into the face-frame stock, I assemble a square-edged face frame first. Then I cut and install a beaded molding on all inside edges. The following five steps will produce a beaded face frame.

1. First, build a standard square-edged face frame. When sizing frame members, remember that the width of the beaded molding will increase the overall width of the stiles and rails.

Installing Beaded Molding in a Face Frame

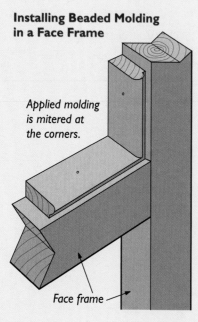

Applied molding is mitered at the corners.

Face frame

Make the beaded molding from straight, clear stock. The molding width should match the face-frame thickness.

2. Mill the beaded molding on a router table, using a beading bit with a 3/16-in. or 1/4-in. radius. As shown in the drawing, the typical profile for this type of molding has a shoulder along one edge. The width of the molding stock should match the thickness of the face frame. (See the drawing and the bottom photo on the facing page.)

3. Cut the beaded molding to rough size so you'll have a single length to fit along the inside of each face-frame member. To "bead" a face-frame opening, start by using a miter saw to make a 45-degree miter cut on one end of one length of molding. Place the mitered end where it will be installed in the face frame, then mark the second miter cut with a sharp pencil. (See the top photo at right.) To take the guesswork out of cutting miters to exact length, secure a wood–auxiliary fence on the miter saw and make both 45-degree cuts in the fence. Now you can place your layout line exactly on the fence miter cut.

4. Using glue and brads, install the molding around the face-frame opening. Only a couple of brads are required for each piece of molding. Take care not to apply too much glue.

5. Repeat this procedure for all face-frame openings.

Place a mitered end in the frame to mark the opposite miter.

Attached to the chopsaw, a wood auxiliary fence lets you align the beaded molding to get an exact miter cut.

Install the mitered molding with glue and brads.

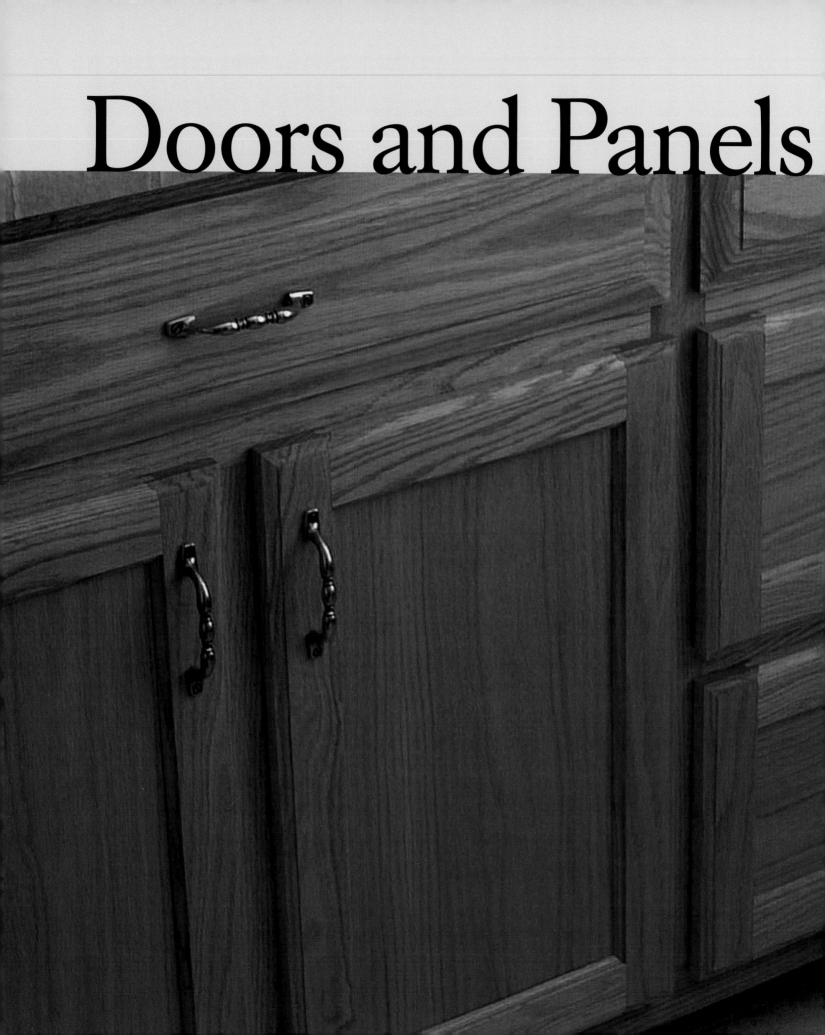

Doors and Panels

CHAPTER FIVE

1 Door Design Options, p. 56

2 Calculating and Cutting Door Parts, p. 58

3 Milling Door Parts, p. 61

4 Assembling Doors, p. 67

5 Building End Panels, p. 71

Cabinet doors are the main attraction in most kitchens. And from a woodworker's point of view, the design and construction of cabinet doors is the most exciting part of building kitchen cabinets.

Most of my customers want frame-and-panel doors on their cabinets. Frame-and-panel doors show off well-crafted joinery as well as the natural beauty of wood. Once you master the basic joinery and panel-raising techniques for door construction, I'll show you how to make doors that have curved panels. This chapter will also cover the construction of end panels, which are built like doors but in larger sizes; they make up a cabinet side that will be visible when the cabinet is installed.

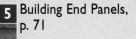

PRO TIP

Get up to speed on different router bits by ordering free catalogs or visiting websites of major suppliers; see Resources on p. 165.

TRADE SECRET

Price and quality vary greatly with router bits. If you need to build only ten or twenty doors for a small kitchen project, cheaper bits should work fine. Buy premium-quality bits if you plan to build cabinets on a regular basis.

WHAT CAN GO WRONG

Calculating exact sizes for cabinet door parts involves plenty of measuring, adding, and subtracting. Miscalculations often aren't discovered until a door is completely assembled. One way to determine exact dimensions quickly and accurately is to use a carpenter's calculator that computes measurements in feet and inches. The Construction Master IV® is a popular model, but others are also available; prices start at around $20.

Door Design Options

Doors and drawer fronts need to be designed together. As you go over the design possibilities covered in this chapter, also refer to the drawer design options explained in Chapter 6.

To design your doors, it's important to understand some door terminology. (See the drawing on the facing page.) The typical frame-and-panel door has five parts. The two vertical frame members are called stiles, and they extend from the bottom to the top of the door. The two horizontal members are called rails. Stiles and rails are usually ¾ in. to ⅞ in. thick. A panel forms the center of the door, and its outer edges are held in slots milled along the inner edges of the stiles and rails. A thin piece of plywood can be used as the door panel. But more often—especially on custom-made cabinets—the panel is made from solid wood. By "raising" the panel, its edges are made thinner so they can fit in the slotted frame. The inner edges of stiles and rails are usually profiled with a router bit or shaper cutter. The "stick" profile is milled along the inner edges of stiles and rails. The ends of the rails need to have a "cope" profile that fits exactly against the stick profile.

There are four basic decisions you have to make when designing cabinet doors. The order given later is not absolutely essential, but it works best in most cases.

1. Determine the stile and rail dimensions. As mentioned earlier, stiles and rails are usually ¾ in. to ⅞ in. thick. Depending on what a customer

Frame-and-Panel Door Styles

There are many design variations possible with frame-and-panel doors. Some of the most popular designs are shown in the drawings at right and below. Once you learn how to make doors with straight stiles and rails, you'll find that curved-top doors are not much more difficult to build. However, curved and cathedral-style doors are usually used on wall cabinets only.

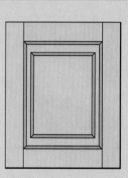

Standard door with raised panel

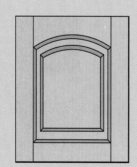

Curved top door with raised panel

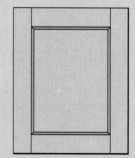

"Shaker Style" door with flat panel

"Cathedral" door with raised panel

wants, I use a width of between 1½ in. and 2½ in. for stiles and rails. Top rails will start out wider than that if you elect to build doors with arched or curved top rails, as shown in the drawings on the facing page.

2. Choose the profile for the stiles and rails. Unless you're building Shaker-style cabinets with plain frame members, you'll need to use router bits or shaper cutters to mill the contoured stick and cope profiles. Manufacturers of router bits and shaper cutters offer a number of different profiles for stiles and rails. As shown in the drawing on p. 58, ogee and quarter-round profiles are popular. I prefer the quarter-round pattern because it's easy to sand and because mullions for glass doors (if they are part of the design) are easy to shape and fit into the frame. For advice on buying door-making bits, see the sidebar on p. 59.

3. Choose the raised-panel profile. There are quite a few raised-panel profiles to choose from. I prefer a simple convex bit because the contoured area can easily be sanded with a random-orbit sander that has been fitted with a contour pad. If you don't have a powerful (at least 3 hp) router equipped with speed control, use a vertical panel-raising bit. If you use a horizontal panel-raising bit, choose one that comes with a back-cutter, which relieves the back of the panel. This moves the front face, or "field," of the panel flush with the frame.

+ SAFETY FIRST

Be sure to wear hearing protection when operating a router. Over time, the high-pitched whine of a router motor will damage unprotected ears.

Frame-and-Panel Joinery Details

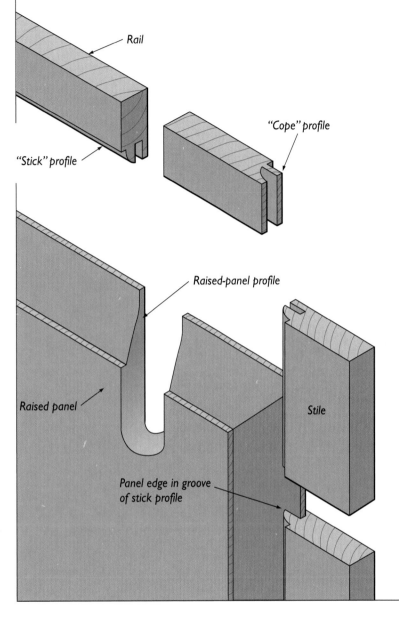

Rail

"Cope" profile

"Stick" profile

Raised-panel profile

Raised panel

Stile

Panel edge in groove of stick profile

Typical Dimensions

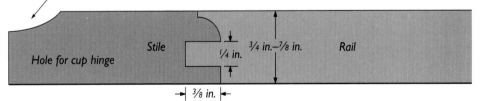

Edge detail cut with raised-panel bit

Hole for cup hinge

Stile

¼ in.

¾ in.–⅞ in.

Rail

⅜ in.

PRO TIP

Cut stiles and rails from clear, straight-grain lumber. Avoid wood with knots and wild grain.

Common Stick (A) and Cope (B) Profiles for Frame-and-Panel Doors

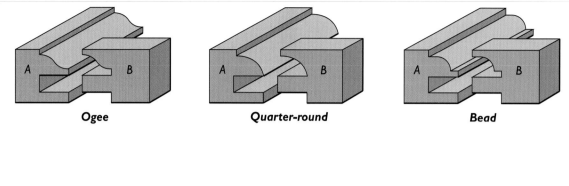

Ogee   **Quarter-round**   **Bead**

Profiles for Raised Panels

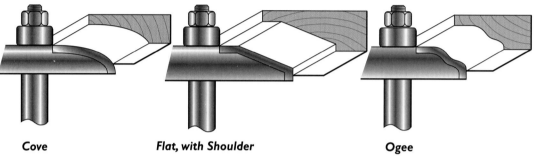

Cove   **Flat, with Shoulder**   **Ogee**

IN DETAIL

When sorting through a lumber supply to make raised panels, cabinetmakers look for wide boards that have a nice color and grain pattern. Inevitably, some of your best-looking wide boards will be warped. But this doesn't make them unusable. A good way to salvage a warped board is to rip it in half, plane both pieces flat, and then glue the board back together. Maintain the grain orientation when you rejoin the boards and it will be hard to tell that you cut the board apart.

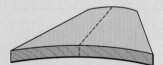

Cut a warped board in half, plane the halves flat, and joint the edges. Then reglue the halves.

4. Determine the outer edge profile. It's not essential to rout a contour around the outside edge of the finished door, but it adds a nice touch. I cut a shallow cove around the door edge, using the small part of a panel-raising bit. The cove is wider than it is deep, which is important if you want to use cup hinges on the door. (See the drawing on p. 57.)

Calculating and Cutting Door Parts

Like the width of stiles and rails, some door measurements are fixed. In the example I use ahead, both stiles and rails are 2¼ in. wide. But stile and rail lengths vary for doors of different sizes, as do panel dimensions. In most of the cabinets I use, the outside dimensions of the door are 1 in. greater than the face-frame opening where the door is installed. This allows for a ½-in. overlay all around the face frame.

Rail length, panel width, and panel height

The length of a door's stiles is always the overall height of the door. To determine the length of the rails and the dimensions of the door panels, use equations based on the finished outside dimensions of each door. For a time-saving trick using those calculations, see the sidebar on p. 60. The equations you need to calculate your door parts are on p. 60:

+ SAFETY FIRST

Because of their weight and diameter, horizontal panel-raising bits should not spin at a router's top speed of 22,000 rpm. To use these bits safely and effectively, your router should be powerful (at least 2 hp) and equipped with variable speed control. This will enable you to run a horizontal panel-raising bit at around 10,000 rpm or at the reduced speed recommended by the manufacturer.

BUYING ROUTER BITS FOR CABINET DOORS

If you don't already have a set of router bits to make raised-panel doors, shopping for new bits can be an adventure. Mail-order and online suppliers offer a staggering variety of router bits, including quite a few bits and bit sets for making cabinet doors. Here are a few tips that will help you find the right bits to match your needs.

Bits for Routing Cope and Stick Profiles in Stiles and Rails

These bits are available in three configurations. No matter which type you decide to buy, make sure the tenon length (and groove depth) is ⅜ in. or ½ in. This will make it much easier to calculate the rail lengths.

- **Matching bits.** One bit cuts the cope profile, the other cuts the stick profile. Although it's more expensive to buy two bits instead of one, a dedicated stick-profile bit is essential if you plan to rout curved rails.

- **Reversible bits.** Such bits can be disassembled, allowing you to reverse the cutters when you need to switch from making cope cuts to making stick cuts. Although economical, a reversible bit is time-consuming and troublesome to use.

- **Stacked bits.** Both cope and stick profiles are stacked together, allowing you to make both cuts simply by changing the height of the cutter in the router table. This type of bit is great for routing straight stiles and rails, but it can't be used on curved rails.

Bits for Raising Panels

The type of bit you buy depends on the router that you will be using.

- **Vertical bits.** Lighter and smaller in diameter than a horizontal bit, a vertical bit is the one to use if your router doesn't have speed control. A high fence needs to be set up to guide the workpiece vertically through the cutter.

- **Horizontal bits.** For safety, this type of bit should spin at around 10,000 rpm, so a router with speed control is necessary.

- **Horizontal bits with back-cutters.** An additional cutter relieves the back of the panel, allowing it to set farther back in the doorframe. Relief cuts can also be made in other ways.

Bits for Cutting Stiles and Rails

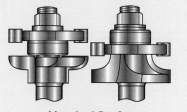

Matched Bit Set

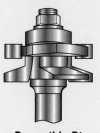

Reversible Bit

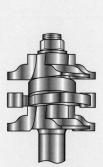

Stacked Bit

Panel-Raising Bits

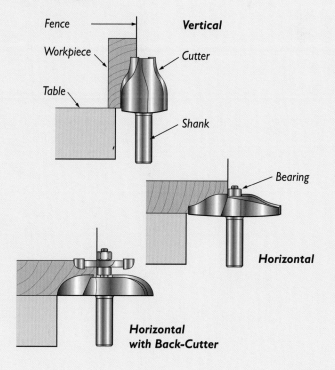

Vertical

Horizontal

Horizontal with Back-Cutter

TRADE SECRET

When planing lumber, try to plane an equal amount of wood from both sides of the board. After running one side of a board through the planer, flip it over and plane the opposite side on the next pass.

TRADE SECRET

If your router is powerful enough to spin horizontal panel-raising and other large bits but lacks speed control, you can buy an add-on variable speed control from MLCS. (See Resources on p. 165.) This accessory plugs into a standard wall outlet and has a dial to control router rpm. The router plugs into the control unit.

A Shop-Made Slide Rule

By making a slide rule from clear plastic, you can greatly speed the task of calculating rail lengths for frame-and-panel doors. A couple of hairlines scribed in the plastic provide the exact difference between the finished width of the door and the required length of the rail. This distance will be constant as long as the stile width remains the same. By adding other lines as necessary, you can also quickly determine the length and width of panels. (See the main text.)

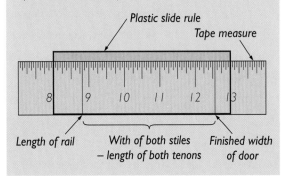

Plastic slide rule
Tape measure
Length of rail
With of both stiles – length of both tenons
Finished width of door

1. **Rail length = Width of door – width of both stiles + length of both tenons.** This formula can be simplified in most cases, since stile and rail width are usually the same in a run of cabinet doors. Tenon length is also constant. Depending on the bits or cutters you have, tenons will probably be either $\frac{3}{8}$ in. or $\frac{1}{2}$ in. long. I'll use $\frac{3}{8}$ in. in the example below.

Example:

Finished width of door:	20
Width of stiles and rails:	$2\frac{1}{4}$
Tenon length:	$\frac{3}{8}$

$$\text{Rail length:} \quad 20 - [(2 \times 2\tfrac{1}{4}) - (2 \times \tfrac{3}{8})]$$
$$= 20 - 3\tfrac{3}{4}$$
$$= 16\tfrac{1}{4}$$

2. **Panel width = Length of rails – allowance for wood movement.** In most cases, an additional $\frac{1}{8}$ in. can be subtracted from rail length to allow the panel to expand without stressing the doorframe. However, you'll need to subtract more if the door panels are wider than

Avoiding Tearout

When planing and jointing boards, you're likely to get tearout if you don't pay attention to the grain direction before running the stock through the thickness planer or over the jointer. This pockmarked wood surface is created when a jointer or planer knife tears wood fibers loose instead of slicing through them. To avoid tearout, check the grain direction of a board and make sure the grain doesn't slant into the cutter. The drawings below show the proper grain orientation for planing and jointing boards.

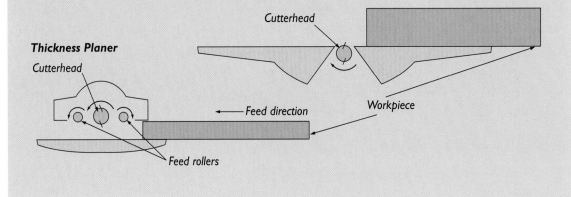

Thickness Planer
Cutterhead
Cutterhead
Workpiece
Feed direction
Feed rollers

18 in. The dryness of the wood and its movement properties also figure in to this calculation. For more details, refer to Chapter 3.

Example:

Rail length: 16¼

Panel width: 16⅛

3. Panel height = Door height – combined rail width + combined groove depth. Because there is very little movement along the grain, no adjustments for movement are necessary.

Making a cutlist

The cabinetry in an average kitchen can have thirty or more doors. If shop space and equipment allow, it's advisable to cut and mill all the door parts before you begin to assemble individual doors. If you work this way, it's essential to have a cutlist to help you keep track of all the parts. Put information like this at the top of your list:

- Door style: Frame and panel with raised panels
- Wood species: Oak
- Stile and rail T × W: ¾ in. × 2¼ in.
- Tenon/Groove: ⅜ in.
- Rail L = Door W − 3¾ in.
- Panel W = Rail L − ⅛ in. Add ⅛ in. for panels more than 20 in. wide.

Once you have this basic information, you can begin to list your parts with their proper dimensions. Each door should have a designated number based on the cabinet where it will be installed. Add other information to the cutlist, such as the perimeter edge detail, the radius of a curved rail, or the glass panel construction. (See the sidebar on pp. 62-63.)

Milling Door Parts

By now, you should have a list of door sizes and door part dimensions. Also, you know the profile of the stiles and rails, how to shape the edges of the doors, and the profile you want on the raised panels. With all this designing and measuring out of the way, its time to get to work in the shop.

1. Preparing stock

Start by sorting through your wood to see which boards should be used for panels, drawer fronts, and frame members. Choose a well-lit spot where you can lay out a good number of boards. Select boards for the panels first. Wide boards that are flat and free of defects are your best candidates, but not all panels can be made from wide stock. If you have to glue up two or three boards to make a panel, make sure the grain and color of the boards match as closely as possible. (See the photo below.) Be prepared to shift and flip boards around until you match the parts of different boards that will look good when glued up into a single panel.

Color and grain pattern are the two most important considerations when choosing boards to glue up into panels.

MAKING GLASS-PANELED DOORS

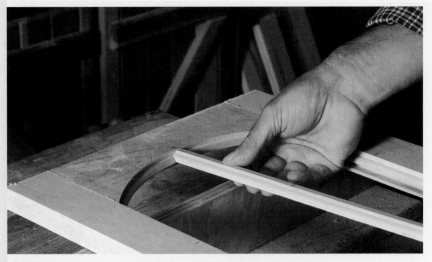

Test-fit each mullion and "creep up" on the final coped length.

Modify the rails of a doorframe by cutting a rabbet where the groove in the stick profile used to be. One way to do this is to use a dado cutter in a table saw, as shown here.

In kitchen cabinets and anywhere else they are used, glasspaneled doors add significantly to cabinetmaking style and craftsmanship. Building these doors involves some painstaking joinery and fitting work, so it's quite an achievement to add them to your cabinetmaking repertoire. Here's how I do it:

A cabinet door that holds a glass panel has an outer frame of stiles and rails, just like a standard frame-and-panel door. Before assembling this type of door, leave the cope cuts on each rail as they are, but cut a rabbet into each rail's "stick" profile, eliminating the groove. For a curved top rail like the one shown in the top photo at left, use a dado blade in your table saw to cut all the way back to the groove on the narrowest section of the rail. (See the center photo at left.) The next step is to glue up the doorframe without the glass installed. To insert the glass later, slide the glass panel all the way into one groove, then halfway into the opposite groove. The panel is held in place with caulk applied to the rabbeted sections of the rails.

Mullions are installed after the doorframe is assembled. The mullions in my glass-paneled doors do not divide the glass into smaller panels but rest against the outside face of the glass. Here's how to cut and install mullions:

Mill the mullion's double roundover profile on the edge of a wide board.

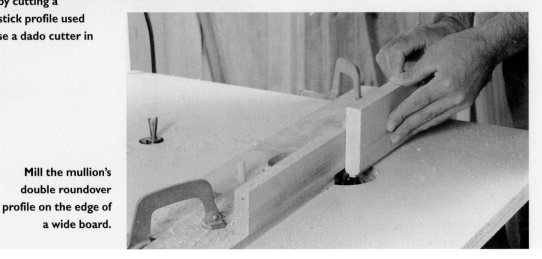

1. Rout the stick profile along both edges of a wide board. Remove the groove cutter from your stick bit for this cut, or use a different bit with the same edge profile. As shown in the bottom photo on the facing page, the mullion profile is a pair of stick profiles routed along the edge of the board.

2. On the table saw, rip the mullion free of the wide board. (See the photo at right.) My mullions are 5/16 in. thick, but this depends on the depth of your stick profile. Always use a push stick for this operation. Repeat the routing and ripping until you have more than enough mullion stock. Extra pieces can be used to replace miscuts.

3. Cut your mullion stock to rough length. Make a cope cut in one end of each piece on the router table, using a section of your cope-cutting bit. To do this, you'll need to make a backing board with the bit, as shown in the left photo below. Secured to the coping jig or sled, the backing board holds each mullion in place as you cope-cut the end. This helps prevent tearout in this tiny piece.

4. Cut and install the mullions, starting with the longest vertical pieces. To get a precise fit with each mullion, lay it in place, mark it, and trim the uncoped end about 1/8 in. long. Go back to the router table, and "creep up" on the final cope cut until the mullion fits snugly in the doorframe. Use this same technique to complete all the mullions. Then glue the assembly together and to the doorframe with clear epoxy glue.

On the table saw, rip the mullion free, taking care to feed the board with the aid of a push stick.

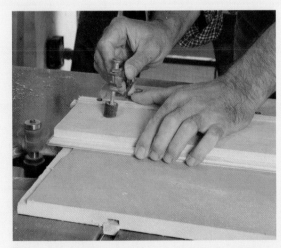

With the mullion held securely in a backing board, cope the mullion's end to fit against the stick profile. You can make these cuts with the same sled used for coping rail ends.

Once the longest mullion is in place, cut and fit the shorter ones. Epoxy the mullion assembly only after all parts fit properly together.

PRO TIP

To reduce the number of passes required on the router table when raising panels, cut part of the waste off the panel edge on the table saw.

TRADE SECRET

Router bits can gum up quickly, and this accumulation of resin reduces cutting effectiveness. To keep bits clean, apply some bit-cleaning compound (available from mail-order suppliers; see Resources on p. 165), then scrub off the residue with an old toothbrush. Household oven cleaner is also an effective bit cleaner.

Space pipe clamps about 12 in. apart, and alternate them under and over the panel.

The panels need to be planed, either before or after they are glued up. If your planer isn't big enough to handle the widest panel in your project, plane all panel stock before gluing up. This ensures that all panels will be the same thickness. Planing will also create a smooth wood surface that requires a minimum of sanding.

I run any board edges that will be glued up through my jointer to make sure they are straight and square. Then I glue panels together with pipe clamps, as shown in the photo at left. Yellow wood glue works fine here, and clamps should be spaced about every 12 in. on alternating sides of the panel. Apply just enough pressure for the glue to squeeze out of the joint. Too much pressure will cup the panel. Since raised panels are not subject to stress or heavy loads, there is no need to strengthen the edge joints with biscuits or dowels. Once the glue has cured completely, you can remove the clamps, scrape off any excess glue, and give each panel a cursory sanding with the random-orbit sander and 120-grit sandpaper. Then cut your panels to the sizes noted on your cutlist.

Drawer fronts are selected next. As when selecting panel stock, avoid wood with eye-catching details. Instead, try to have the grain and color of the drawer fronts match the grain and color of the nearby panels.

What is left of the lumber pile is cut into stile and rail stock. I rip stile and rail pieces to rough width (about ⅛ in. over) so that I can run them on edge through my thickness planer. This removes saw marks from the edges and creates a uniform width on all pieces. As you rip boards to width, you may notice that some boards bend or twist after they've been cut. This can happen when cutting releases internal stresses in the wood. Instead of discarding a longer piece that is bowed or twisted, try to cut a few short rails from straighter parts of the board. Always cut your longest frame members first to make sure you will have enough straight stock on hand. Use your planer again to plane all frame stock to a uniform thickness, then cut stiles and rails to the finished lengths noted on your cutlist.

2. Shaping stile and rail stock

The cope cuts on the ends of rails are always done first, even on curved rails. The safest way to do this is with a jig that clamps the rail against a backing

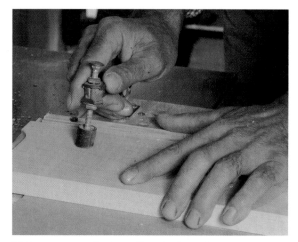

Make cope cuts in the rail ends first. Use a shop-made sled to keep the rail clamped in position and provide backing where the bit exits the workpiece. The sled can ride in the miter slot of the router or shaper table, as shown here, or it can run against a fence secured to the table.

board. The jig can be guided against the fence on your router table or shaper, or it can slide in a miter slot if your table is equipped with one. (See the bottom photo on the facing page.)

After all cope cuts are done, it's time to cut the stick or pattern profile along the inner edges of the stiles and rails. If your router bit (or shaper cutter) cuts the full thickness of the material, the outfeed fence will have to be offset slightly from the infeed fence to support the slightly reduced width of the workpiece. (See the photo at right.)

If you are building curved-top doors, the stick profile also needs to be cut along the curved edge of each top rail. To do this safely and accurately, attach a template to the top rail, as shown in the photo below. For details on making templates for curved rails, see the sidebar on pp. 68–69.

3. Shaping raised panels

The router setup for shaping raised panels is pretty straightforward. If you are using a vertical panel-raising bit, raise the bit to cut the full width of the profile, positioning the fence to hide most of the cutter so you can "creep up" on the final profile in successive passes. Make sure you set up a fence

Guide stiles and rails against a fence to cut the stick profile. Because this router bit cuts the full thickness of the material, the outfeed fence needs to be offset slightly.

that is at least 8 in. high to support the panel vertically as you guide it through the cutter.

Since I have a powerful router with variable speed control, I prefer to use a horizontal panel-raising bit, which is the only type of bit that will raise a curved-top panel. To set up for using a horizontal bit, adjust the router table fence so the cutter is set to cut the full width of the profile. The bit's ball-bearing guide should be in line with

As you rout the stick profile in a curved-top rail, the bit's bearing rides against a curved template attached to the workpiece.

IN DETAIL

When using a horizontal panel-raising bit on the router table, keep the fence position the same for every cut, but gradually increase the height of the bit to attain the final profile. A different setup is required when using a horizontal bit with a back-cutter. Start cutting with the bit set to its final height but with the fence covering most of the bit, as shown in the top drawing below. For the final pass, set the fence flush with the bearing located between the cutters. The edge of the panel runs against the fence and the bearing.

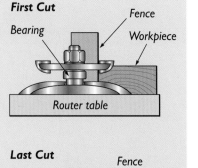

First Cut
Bearing · Fence · Workpiece
Router table

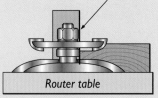

Last Cut
Fence
Router table

A wide, low fence works well when raising panels with a horizontal bit. Cut the profile in stages, increasing the bit's cutting depth with each pass.

A panel with a simple curve at the top can be routed with a straight fence. Make sure the bearing on top of the bit runs against the curved edge.

Remove the outfeed fence to raise a panel with a compound curve at the top. Keep the bearing in contact with the curved edge.

the front face of the fence. Then lower the cutter to take only a small bite. Run all straight panel edges through this setup with your router speed reduced to around 10,000 rpm. After the first pass, raise the cutter slightly, then make another pass to remove a little more material.

The depth of cut you use depends on the density of the wood. With softwoods, such as pine and fir, you can get your finished profile in several passes. More passes and shallower cuts will be necessary with hardwoods, such as oak and maple. Make your last pass the lightest pass; you'll get smoother results if you just remove a small amount of material. (See the top photo on the facing page.)

Raising curved panels. If your panel-raising bit is equipped with a pilot bearing, you can make curved raised panels without much fuss. Trace the curve from the rail template onto the panel that needs a matching curved top, then cut the curve with a jigsaw or bandsaw. Since the edges of the raised panels will be hidden in the grooves of the doorframe, they do not have to be perfectly smooth. Just give the cut edge a quick sanding to smooth it.

A panel with a single curve can be shaped with the full fence in place on your router table. Start at one end of the curve, and keep the edge of the panel running against the ball bearing on the top of the bit. (See the center photo on the facing page.) To raise the edge of a compound curve, remove the outfeed fence, or simply install a half fence on the infeed side of the bit. Start cutting where a straight edge of the panel meets the curved edge, move the edge of the workpiece against the bearing, and keep running the edge against the bearing until the complete curve has been cut. (See the bottom photo on the facing page.) As with basic rectangular panels, it's best to make at least several passes until you reach the full profile.

Assembling Doors

Before the door parts are glued together, they need to be sanded to smooth out any burn or milling marks, especially in areas that will be difficult to reach after assembly. This can be done entirely by hand or with the help of power tools. A sanding sponge can make hand-sanding easier. (See the top photo below.) My preferred method is a sanding wheel mounted on a drill press. (See the bottom photo below.) The wheel I use is 2 in. thick by 10 in. in diameter. It's made up of hundreds of small sanding strips that follow the contours of a profile. Depending on the grit of the sandpaper and the rpm of the wheel, this method

A foam-core sanding sponge easily conforms to a simple roundover profile.

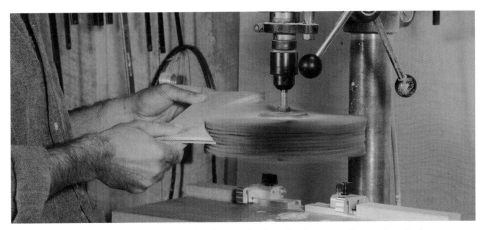

Chucked in a drill press, a sanding wheel contains hundreds of sanding strips that can smooth almost any profile. Here, a stile is being sanded.

TRADE SECRET

To make details easy to duplicate, keep an offcut record of each cabinetmaking project. Mill the different profiles in scrap stock of an appropriate thickness before changing each router table setup. In addition to the cope and stick profile and raised-panel profile used to make cabinet doors, keep a record of the profile used on the outside edges of doors and drawer fronts.

Spaceballs

Keeping the panel centered and rattle-free has always been a problem with raised-panel doors. As a panel shrinks during the heating season, it fits more loosely in the grooved doorframe. This can cause the panel to rattle in its frame or expose unfinished edge areas. Spaceballs™ were developed to overcome these problems. (See Resources on p. 165.) These resilient, .26-in.-dia. balls can easily be inserted in a typical ¼-in.-wide, ⅜-in.-deep panel groove during door assembly. By compressing and expanding as the panel shrinks and swells, Spaceballs keep the panel centered and rattle-free. If your wood has a high moisture content (around 12%), the panel should compress the Spaceballs significantly. With dry wood, the fit should leave your spacers closer to full size. When using Spaceballs at the top and bottom edges of the panel, subtract an additional ³⁄₁₆ in. from the panel's height to make room for the spacers.

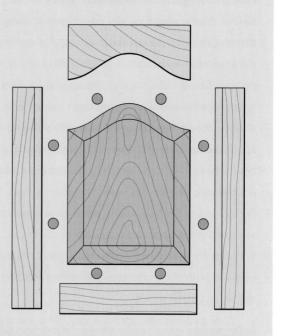

Driving a couple of ½-in. brads into the stile-and-rail joint enables you to remove and reuse the clamps.

can be very aggressive. I never sand the part of the stiles where the rails will join.

When gluing up a door, spread glue on only the coped rail ends and the section of the stiles where the rails will fit. Keep glue off the panel and out of the groove where the panel edges will fit. If you have trouble keeping the panels centered in their frames, consider using Spaceballs, as explained in the sidebar above. Position each clamp in line with a rail, and apply light clamping pressure to close the cope-and-stick joints. Make sure the doorframe sets flat and check it for squareness. Tack each cope-and-stick joint fast by driving a couple of ½-in. brads from the back of the door, then remove the clamps so they can be used on the next assembly. (See the photo at left.)

Let the glue cure for at least a couple of hours before you begin the final sanding. I start out using 120-grit sandpaper in my random-orbit sander. Then I edge the outside of the doorframe. Finally, I finish sanding with 220-grit paper, taking time to hand-sand the edges after going over flat areas with the random-orbit sander.

Building End Panels

Solid wood end panels give any kitchen a unique appearance. When factory-made cabinets are ordered, the exposed cabinet sides are made from a piece of plywood that is finished to match the cabinet doors, drawers, and face frames. When you build your own cabinets, these exposed sides or ends can be frame-and-panel assemblies made from solid wood, just like the cabinet doors and drawer fronts. As shown in the photo above, the finished appearance is much more striking, and the higher level of craftsmanship is definitely apparent.

These assemblies can be used on the exposed sides of wall and base cabinets, on full-height pantry cabinets, as an enclosure panel for the refrigerator, and as a back panel on a kitchen island. If you are building your own doors, you already have all the tools and equipment you need to build end panels. To learn how to use end panels in assembling cabinet cases, see Chapter 7.

An end panel is a frame-and-panel assembly, just like a cabinet door. It can contain a single panel or several panels, depending on its size and design. (See the drawing at right.) When your cabinetry is installed, an end panel should appear to be well integrated with the cabinet doors and drawer fronts, so plan to use the same wood throughout. It's also important for end panels to have the same symmetry and proportions used in cabinet doors. When designing a tall end panel for the side of a pantry cabinet, locate the panel rails

You can construct a cabinet end panel like this one using the same joinery techniques as those for frame-and-panel doors. I incorporate another special feature here: a 45-degree corner board embellished with rosettes and flutes.

End Panel Design for a Base Cabinet

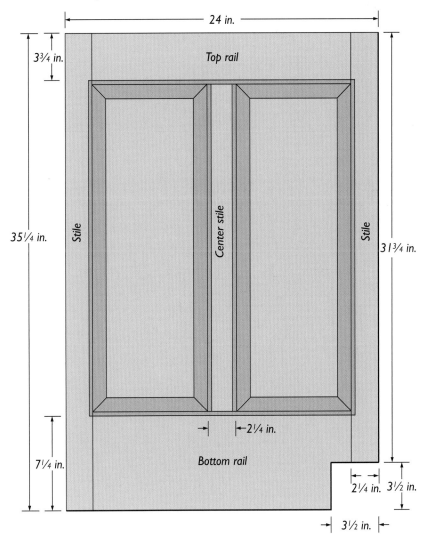

24 in.

3¾ in.

Top rail

35¼ in.

Stile

Center stile

Stile

31¾ in.

2¼ in.

7¼ in.

Bottom rail

2¼ in.   3½ in.

3½ in.

TRADE SECRET

Although it takes extra time during the door-construction process, applying a sealer coat or even completely finishing door panels before they are permanently assembled in their frames is a smart thing to do. This step ensures that each panel gets complete edge-to-edge finish coverage, which isn't possible when finishing happens after door assembly.

to continue the horizontal lines established along the front of the cabinetry.

When an end panel joins the cabinet face frame at a 90-degree angle, make sure you size the end panel's outer stile so that the stile widths will be equal at the outside corner. When I design end panels, I like to incorporate a 45-degree corner, as shown in the drawings below. When using this special treatment, make sure that the added space taken up by the corner doesn't extend the cabinet beyond its planned location. I recommend drawing a full-scale plan view of the corner. This will give you an exact measurement that shows how much extra space is taken up by the corner.

Building an End Panel with a 45-Degree Corner

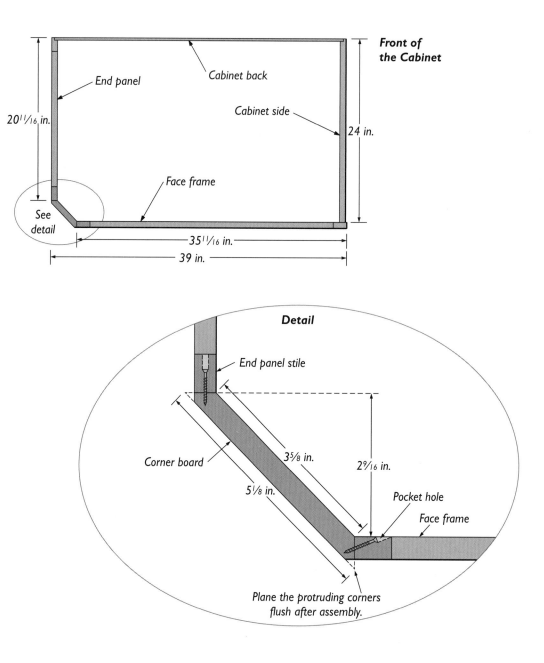

The corner board is a clear, straight-grained piece with 45-degree bevel cuts on both long edges. To make those cuts safely and accurately, see the sidebar at right. As you'll see in Chapter 7, the 45-degree edges make it easy to glue and screw the corner board to the end panel and to the cabinet face frame. After cutting the corner board to its final dimensions, I give it some ornamentation—rosettes cut near the top and bottom of the board, with flutes extending between them. I cut the rosettes with a rosette cutter chucked in my drill press. The flutes can be cut with a router and a round-nose bit (also called a core-box bit). I prefer to chuck this bit in my drill press and run it at slower speed to avoid burning the wood. (See the photo below.)

To cut decorative flutes in a corner board, you can chuck a round-nose router bit in the drill press and guide the board against a fence.

Cutting a Panel with Two Bevels

The panel that forms a 45-degree corner between the face frame and the base cabinet side or end panel requires 45-degree bevel cuts along both long edges. To make these bevel cuts accurately and safely, follow these steps:

1. Tilt your table saw blade 45 degrees and test this setting for accuracy by making trial cuts in scrap material, then fitting the two bevel cuts together. They should form a right angle. Adjust the blade tilt, if necessary.

2. Make the first cut by guiding the workpiece and a ¼-in. hardboard sled through the blade. As shown in the drawing below, the hardboard sled will prevent the waste piece from being pulled down by the spinning blade into the throat plate's opening.

3. Adjust the rip fence to cut the workpiece to its finished width, and make the second cut using the sled, as before.

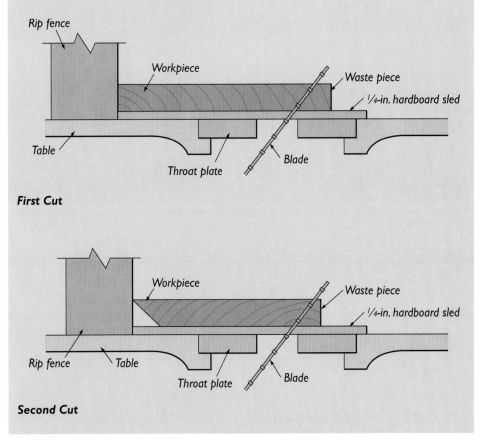

First Cut

Second Cut

Building

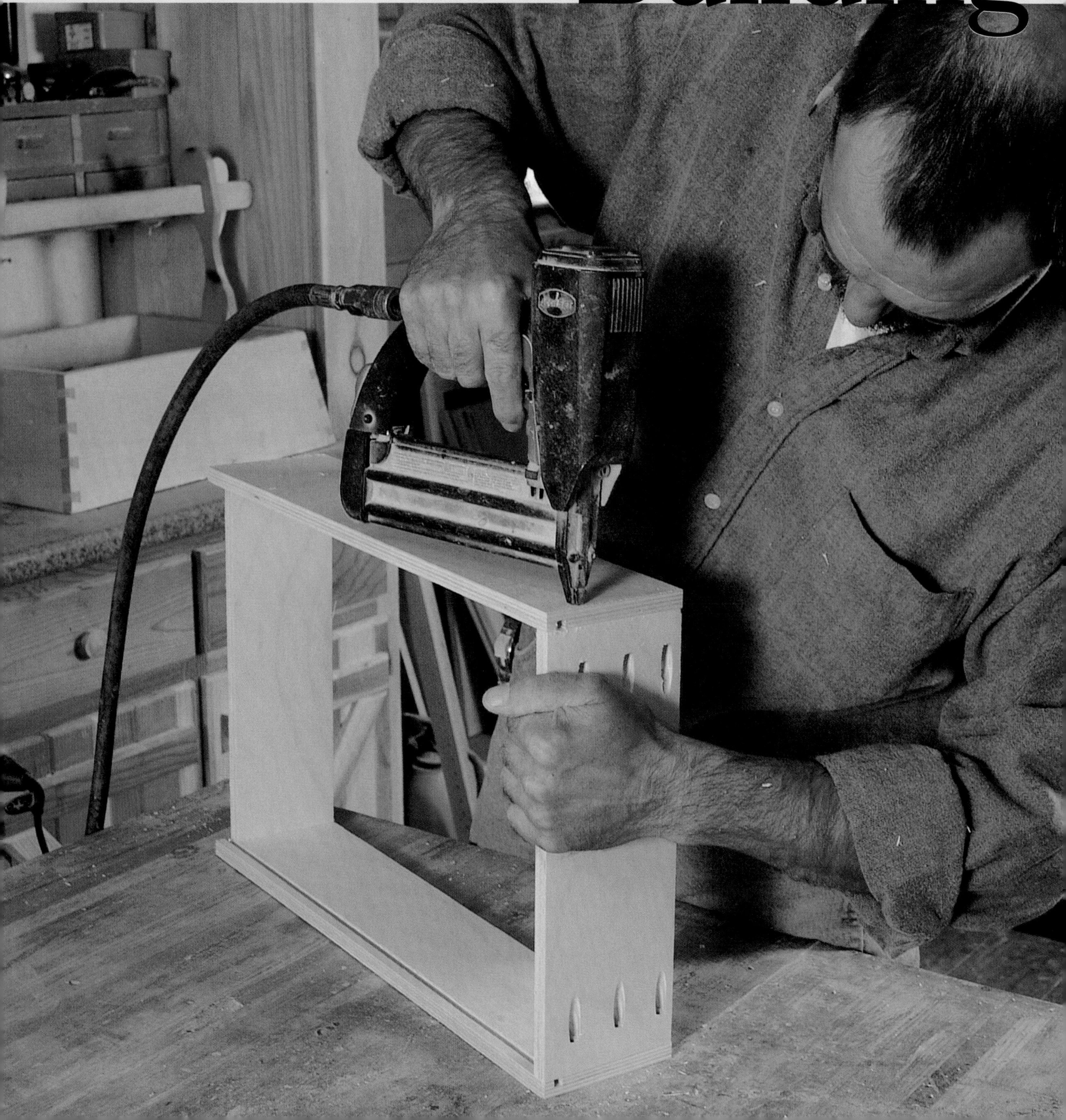

CHAPTER SIX

Drawers

1 Style, Joinery, and Materials, p. 76

Drawers play an important role in the finished appearance of kitchen cabinetry. When cabinets are well designed, the overall impression is a pleasing combination of doors and drawer fronts. But the drawers in a kitchen also have to work hard every day, enduring more use and heavier loads than those used in chests, dressers, and other types of furniture.

Thanks to the heavy-duty slide hardware that is available today, many homeowners are choosing cabinets with extra-large drawers instead of doors. These oversize drawers offer improved convenience for storing large pots and pans. For more information on drawer-slide hardware, see Chapter 11. In this chapter, I'll cover drawer design options, materials for building drawer boxes and fronts, and joinery details in drawer construction.

2 Building a Basic Drawer Box, p. 78

3 Building a Dovetailed Drawer, p. 81

4 Making Drawer Fronts, p. 83

PRO TIP

When selecting wood for applied fronts, take the time to choose attractive stock that is compatible with the wood used to make the cabinet doors.

IN DETAIL

Dovetail drawer joints were first used on furniture in the mid-1600s. Woodworkers developed distinctive styles and methods for creating dovetails, making this joinery detail synonymous with top-quality craftsmanship. Today, furniture factories have machines that produce dovetail joints in seconds. Traditional woodworkers still pride themselves on dovetails that are cut by hand. But in many small cabinet shops, a wide range of dovetail jigs and carbide-tipped router bits are used to duplicate the look of handcrafted dovetails quickly and precisely.

Sanding the drawer is much easier without the bottom panel installed.

After prefinishing the drawer bottom, slide it into the grooves milled in the front and sides.

Complete the drawer assembly by screwing the bottom to the bottom edge of the back.

5. **Sand and finish the drawer box.** At this stage, your partially assembled drawers are very easy to sand and finish. (See the top left photo above.) I prefer to finish drawer boxes with a clear polyurethane or catalyzed lacquer. Unless you are using prefinished plywood bottoms, now is the time to finish those parts as well.

6. **Install the drawer bottoms.** Slide the bottom into place from the back of the drawer box, as shown in the top right photo above. Then hold the assembly square as you drill countersunk pilot holes for several ⅝-in. screws. (See the bottom photo above.)

Building a Dovetailed Drawer

If your aim is to build a masterpiece, then you need to assemble your drawer boxes with dovetail joints. This means investing in a dovetail jig and the one or two bits designed for it. You can buy a jig and a single bit for cutting half-blind dovetails for less than $100. More advanced jig and bit sets can cost $300 or more. The good news is that once you learn how to use this equipment, you'll have no trouble turning out a full-kitchen's worth of top-quality drawers.

The Katie Jig® that I use costs about $250 and is designed to be used with a router table or hand-held router. The jig enables you to cut through dovetails with variable spacing. Because the jig can be repositioned easily on wide stock, it can also be used to make dovetailed chests and other furniture. As with other through-dovetail jigs, a pattern-cutting bit is required to cut the pins. To cut the tails, use a dovetail bit guided by a pilot bearing.

The Katie Jig's only disadvantage is that it works best with two routers—one for the pattern-cutting bit and one for the dovetail bit. By mounting two routers in my router table, I can dovetail all the parts for one drawer in less than 10 minutes. That's about the same time as it takes to assemble a drawer with pocket joinery. With just a single router table setup, it can take a little longer. Here's how I build a dovetailed drawer using a dovetail jig:

1. Cut the parts to size. Assuming that your drawer parts are ¾ in. thick, the cutting depth for both bits should be $^{13}/_{16}$ in. This will leave $^1/_{16}$ in. to trim on each side of the finished box. Make the length of the drawer sides, front, and back ⅛ in. greater than the finished outside dimensions of the drawer. Dovetail joints should always

start with a half-pin at the edges. To achieve this, you may have to adjust the height of the drawer box slightly.

2. Lay out and mark the parts. Mark each corner 1, 2, 3, and 4 on both boards. The front and back will have pins, so mark them that way. Also, write "top" on the top of the drawer and mark the inside of each drawer part.

3. Adjust the stop blocks. Position the blocks to center the drawer parts on the jig. Remember that each side should start with

When the box's sides, front, and back are in their proper orientation, number each corner and mark the inside face of each piece.

The adjustable stop blocks on the top of the jig keep one side and one end of the box positioned over the aluminum guides.

WHAT CAN GO WRONG

Even with careful measuring, calculating, and assembly, it's still possible for drawers to be slightly off in their finished width, making it impossible to install the drawer with standard slide hardware. If the drawer box is too narrow by 1/8 in. or so, you can shim out one or both sides. If the box is too wide by 1/8 in. or so, raise the blade on the table saw to the installed height of the slide hardware.

First remove any nails or screws to avoid cutting into metal with your saw, then guide the drawer box against the rip fence to cut off a small amount from both sides. (See the photo below.) If the drawer box is more than 1/8 in. too small or too big, make a new one in the correct size.

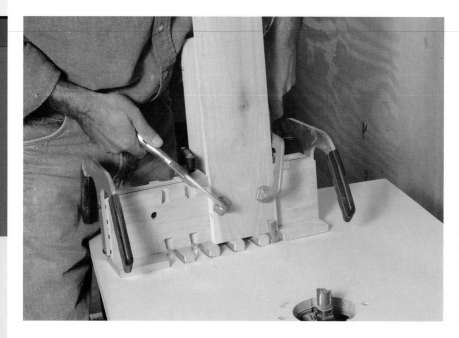

I set up two routers in my router table. One has a pattern bit that is used on the pin side of the jig. A dovetail bit is used on the tail side.

With its dovetails completed and its bottom groove cut, this drawer box is ready for final sanding and assembly.

Slide the bottom into place after joining the front and back to one side, then glue the remaining side in place.

about half a pin. Use a square to make sure the stop blocks are square.

4. Clamp the drawer parts on the jig. Always position the inside part of the board against the jig's backing board. Place the pin board on the pin-cutting side of the jig and the tail board on the opposite side, then clamp both parts to the jig.

5. Cut the pin and tail joints. Use the pattern bit on the pin side of the jig and the dovetail bit on the tail side. When you're done with one set of ends, flip the stock and repeat the process. Then repeat this cutting sequence with the remaining drawer side and end.

6. Test-fit the parts. See whether the joints fit snugly and check the outside dimensions of the drawer box.

7. Cut the bottom groove. Cut a groove for the bottom in the sides, front, and back pieces. Locate the groove so that it is centered on

Check the box for square before setting it aside so the glue can dry.

If you have distinguished grain or color patterns in your cabinet doors, select wood for the drawer fronts with the same characteristics.

a pin. The groove will show on the outside of the completed drawer box, but you'll cover it with the applied front and the slide hardware.

8. Glue up the box. Give all drawer parts a final sanding, then apply glue and assemble the box, taking care to check it for square. I like to lay a drawer side on the table, spread glue on the pins, and then push the back and front into the drawer side. Then I slide the bottom panel into its groove and add the final side. Clamps aren't necessary if the corner joints fit snugly.

9. Trim the corners. If the pins and tails stand proud, you'll need to trim them flush. You can do this quickly using a flush-trim bit in your router.

Making Drawer Fronts

With the boxes finished, it's time to turn your attention to the applied drawer fronts. As discussed at the beginning of this chapter, I build two types of drawer fronts: solid wood fronts and frame-and-panel fronts made just like cabinet doors. The frame-and-panel fronts are used primarily on deep drawers. Both types are attached to the

drawer box by driving screws from inside the box. I'll cover the installation process in Chapter 12, when I discuss drawer handles, pulls, and other hardware.

In the finished installation, the cabinets should have drawers that look good individually and together, with a pleasing overall composition of wood color and grain. Select the wood for drawer fronts carefully; you'll appreciate this extra attention when the job is done. (See the photo above.)

The outside dimensions of the drawer front should be 1 in. greater than the drawer's face-frame opening. See Chapter 4 for instructions on building frame-and-panel assemblies. When you have cut the solid wood fronts to their finished sizes and completed the frame-and-panel fronts, it's time to rout a decorative edge detail around the outside edges of each front. For a very basic edge treatment, use a chamfer, roundover, or beading bit in the router. I like the look of doing this edge detail with a panel-raising bit.

Base Cabinets

CHAPTER SEVEN

1 Making a Cutlist, p. 86

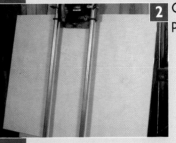

2 Cutting Panels to Size, p. 87

Whichever techniques are used to build cabinet cases, the result is always the same: a box made from plywood or other sheet material, designed to have doors, drawers, or a combination of both. In this chapter, I'll show you how to build three types of kitchen base cabinets: standard base cabinets, corner cabinets, and end cabinets.

3 Assembling Standard Base Cabinets, p. 87

To get to this stage, you need to complete the face frames for your base cabinets, as described in Chapter 4. The frames define the openings for the doors and drawers and determine the dimensions of your base cabinets.

4 Building Corner Base Cabinets, p. 91

The method I use to build cabinet cases yields a beautiful, strong, finished product without any complex or time-consuming joinery work. The case is held together with screws, biscuits, and a few finishing nails. If you can drive these nails with a brad driver, instead of by hand, the work will go faster.

5 Building End Panel Cabinets, p. 94

TRADE SECRET

A good labeling system is essential when you are cutting and assembling a series of cabinets. Without proper labeling, it's easy for parts to get mixed up and end up in the wrong cabinets. The labeling system used by cabinet manufacturers is useful and easy to understand. The letter "W" denotes a wall cabinet. "B" is for base cabinets, "P" stands for pantry, and "C" is a corner unit. "BC" is a base corner cabinet and "SB" denotes a sink base. The number following the letter is the width of the cabinet. Some examples: B32 is a base cabinet that is 32 in. wide. W18 is a wall cabinet that is 18 in. wide.

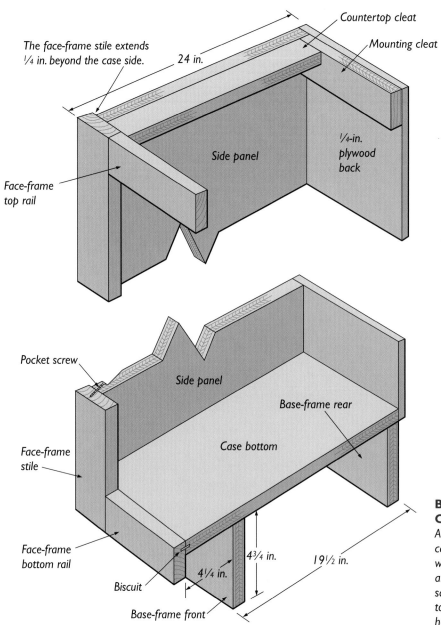

Countertop cleat

The face-frame stile extends ¼ in. beyond the case side.

24 in.

Mounting cleat

Side panel

¼-in. plywood back

Face-frame top rail

Pocket screw

Side panel

Base-frame rear

Face-frame stile

Case bottom

Face-frame bottom rail

Biscuit

4¼ in.

4¾ in.

19½ in.

Base-frame front

Base Cabinet Cutaway
A standard base cabinet can be built in different widths, but the depth and height remain the same. Join the parts together with butt joints held fast with biscuits, screws, and brads.

Making a Cutlist

As shown in the drawing above, base cabinet joinery details are very simple. Certain base cabinet dimensions remain the same, even when cabinets are built in different widths. For example, standard base cabinets are 35¼ in. high, not including the countertop. Cabinet depth, including the face frame, is uniform at 24 in. If your base cabinet's face frames are complete (see Chapter 4), you have all the information necessary to generate a cutlist for your case parts. (See the sidebar on the facing page.) Once you have listed all the parts and their dimensions, you can figure out the easiest and most economi-

Making a Cabinet Cutlist

The designation "B36" identifies this case as a base cabinet (B) that's 36 in. wide. The 36-in. width refers to the face frame. The width of the cabinet case is ¹/₂ in. less than the width of the face frame. The cutlist for this cabinet is shown below.

B36 dimensions: Width (W) 36 in.; height (H) 35¹/₄ in.; depth (D) 24 in.

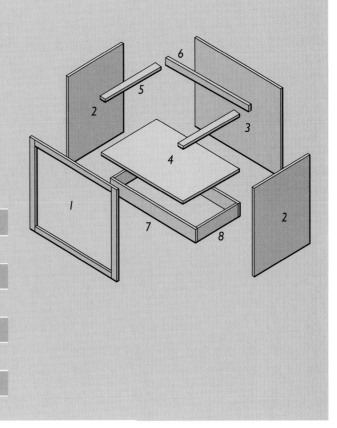

Part ID	Name	Qty.	Dimensions	Notes
(1)	Face frame	1	36 × 31³/₄ × ³/₄	
(2)	Side panel	2	23 × 30¹/₂ × ³/₄	
(3)	Back panel	1	35¹/₂ × 30¹/₂ × ¹/₄	Panel width = W − ¹/₂ in.
(4)	Floor panel	1	23 × 34 × ³/₄	Panel width = W − 2 in.
(5)	Countertop cleat	2	22¹/₄ × 2 × ³/₄	
(6)	Mounting cleat	1	34 × 2 × ³/₄	Cleat length = W − 2 in.
(7)	Base front and back	2	35¹/₂ × 4³/₄ × ³/₄	Length = W − ¹/₂ in.
(8)	Base sides	2	18 × 4³/₄ × ³/₄	

cal way to cut them from standard 4×8 plywood panels.

Cutting Panels to Size

To build cabinets, you need to have an accurate, efficient way to cut plywood panels and other sheet material. Some cabinet shops use a panel cutter—a circular saw that can slide up and down on a vertical track. In other shops (like mine, for example), most of the panel cutting is done on a powerful cabinet saw equipped with a sliding table and a laminate-topped outfeed table. For more options on cutting panels safely and accurately, see the sidebar on p 89.

I prefer to cut the largest parts first (sides, bottoms, and backs), then work my way toward the smaller parts. You can cut the sides and bottoms for all standard base cabinets with your table saw's rip fence set 23 in. from the blade. It's smart not to

change this setting until you've cut all the case pieces that are 23 in. wide.

As you cut each part, label it. It takes just a few seconds to write the name of the part in an area that won't be seen once the cabinet is assembled. (See the Trade Secret on the facing page.) Keep the parts for individual cabinets stacked together.

Assembling Standard Base Cabinets

After all the parts are cut to size, assemble the case. A workbench provides a flat, solid work surface for this job, but some cabinetmakers prefer to use a low assembly table. (See the sidebar on p. 88.)

1. Assemble the base frame. This frame can go together with butt joints, and the fasteners don't need to be hidden, as they'll be

TRADE SECRET

For smooth cuts in plywood, use an 80-tooth melamine blade in your table saw. A triple-chip grind provides good results. It's also a good idea to use a zero-clearance throat plate in your table saw. By supporting the stock right up to the blade, the throat plate helps prevent chip-out. See Resources on p. 165.

IN DETAIL

After the base cabinets are installed, their base frames will be completely covered by a continuous kickplate. Because of this, you don't have to be fussy about which stock is used to make base frame members. Solid wood and plywood are both acceptable, as long as the frame members are straight and at least 3/4 in. thick.

Cabinet case construction starts with assembling the base frame.

covered later. The base frame for a standard base cabinet has four frame members, all of which are 4¾ in. high. The length of the front and back frame members equals the finished width of the cabinet case. The side members are 18 in. long. When I have a cabinet more than 36 in. wide, I also install a center frame member. Don't forget to drill pocket holes in the side of each frame piece. That way, you'll be able to fasten the side frame pieces to the cabinet sides. I use a nailer to assemble the frame quickly. (See the photo at left.) Then I reinforce each joint with a couple of 1⅝-in. drywall screws. Drill countersunk pilot holes to avoid having the screws split the wood.

2. Attach the cabinet's floor panel to the base. This step strengthens and squares up the base. Drive pocket screws in the holes you drilled earlier to fasten the front and back base pieces to

Make an Assembly Table

Assembling cabinet cases requires a broad work surface that's dead flat, solid, and at a good working height. Although a good workbench will do, some cabinet-makers prefer to build a low assembly table from plywood and dimension lumber. The drawing shows a basic design; you can adjust the dimensions to fit your needs. Mount some heavy-duty locking casters on the table base so you can move it out of the way when it's not in use. The space beneath the top comes in handy for storing lumber, pipe clamps,

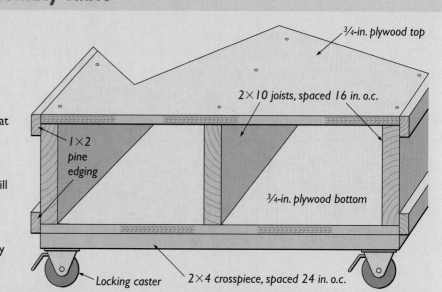

and other items. To prevent splintering, cover exposed plywood edges with solid wood trim. Finish the work surface with a couple coats of polyurethane varnish. This makes it easy to sweep clean and allows dried glue to be scraped off easily.

SAFE, ACCURATE WAYS TO CUT PLYWOOD AND OTHER SHEET MATERIALS

Commercial cabinet shops have special equipment for cutting 4×8 sheets of plywood and other composite panels to their exact sizes. In a more modestly equipped workshop, it can be challenging to transform a full-size sheet of ³/₄-in. plywood into precisely cut backs, sides, and bottoms. Here are some tips you can use to do the job safely and accurately:

- **First, get help, if you can.** A ³/₄-in.-thick sheet of plywood is heavy and difficult to move. A helper can make the job safer and easier.

- **Take advantage of "factory" edges.** You can usually count on straight edges in full-size panels, thanks to close manufacturing tolerances. Check for straightness by eye or with a steel straightedge. A straight factory edge is a reliable reference edge for laying out cabinet parts.

- **Cut pieces to rough (or final) size with a circular saw.** By cutting a case part about ¹/₈ in. oversize with a circular saw, you will have a smaller piece of plywood to cut to its final size on the table saw. You can also cut parts to their final sizes with a circular saw, if you learn how to guide the base of the saw against a straightedge clamped to the plywood. Use a fine-tooth, finish-cutting blade in the circular saw, and adjust the saw's depth of cut to about ¹/₈ in. deeper than the panel's thickness. To set up for cutting a full-size sheet, support the sheet on several 8-ft. 2×4s placed on the floor.

- **Make a short rip fence longer.** The standard rip fence on a contractor's saw or benchtop saw may not be long enough to guide a long piece of plywood. Extend the fence by screwing a straight wooden auxiliary fence to the stock fence.

- **Run the straightest edge against the rip fence.** Plan your cuts so that you're always running a straight, true edge against the rip fence.

- **Set up outfeed support.** If you have room in your shop, build a laminate-top outfeed table for your table saw. (See the photo below.) The level of the table should be about ¹/₈ in. below the top surface of the table saw. Or set up outfeed rollers to support the stock as it leaves the saw.

- **Equip your table saw with a sliding table.** If you need to cut plywood and other sheet material on a regular basis, consider buying a sliding table for your table saw. Different aftermarket versions are available; see Resources on p. 165. Although it's an expensive accesssory, a sliding table makes it possible for a solo woodworker to make exact cuts in large sheet material.

TRADE SECRET

Because of the high cost of cabinet-grade plywood, it's important to obtain the optimum number of parts from every panel you use. Panel layout software is a smart choice if you like to generate your cutlists on the computer. But graph paper is also a workable strategy. Make sure your cutlist is complete before you begin to divide sheets of plywood into case parts. This will enable you to lay out the cuts for all the parts you need, including small pieces such as braces and cleats.

WHAT CAN GO WRONG

Edges and corners can become damaged in the course of handling a plywood panel. When this happens, a section of the panel becomes unusable. Always inspect a panel carefully (the edges, corners, and "show" face) before cutting cabinet parts. Damaged sections can often be avoided through a well-planned layout. To protect plywood panels from damage, store them away from the main traffic area of your workshop, and make sure the edges rest on 2×4 sleepers rather than on a concrete floor.

Drive pocket screws to fasten the base frame to the floor panel.

The side panel butts against the edge of the floor panel and rests on the top edge of the base assembly's side piece. I attach the side panel with biscuits and screws.

Biscuit joints help align the face frame's bottom rail with the floor panel. I fasten the face-frame stiles to the case sides by driving pocket screws from inside the case.

the cabinet's floor panel. (See the top left photo above.) If you are building a drawer base rather than a door base, it's not necessary to hide the fasteners when joining the base to the bottom. Instead, you can simply drive screws through the top of the panel and into the top edges of the base.

3. Drill pocket holes near the front outside edge of each side panel. This will enable you to screw the side panels to the stiles of the face frame. Four pocket holes along each edge should be adequate. Use a plate joiner to mill several biscuit slots along the side and front edges of the bottom panel. Mill matching slots in the face frame's bottom rail and near the bottom edge of each side panel. In addition to strengthening the bottom panel's connection to the case sides and face frame, biscuit joints help keep the parts properly aligned.

4. Attach the sides to the base frame and bottom panel. Spread glue on the biscuit joints, then reinforce the joint with screws. (See the top right photo on the facing page.)

5. Attach the face frame. As mentioned earlier, use glue and biscuits where the face frame's bottom rail joins the case bottom. (See the bottom photo on the facing page.) To help hold the face frame against the case sides until you can drive pocket screws, shoot a finishing nail through each stile and into the cabinet side. Drive each nail near the top corner of the stile, where it will be hidden after the countertop is installed.

6. Install the cleats. Drive a couple of finishing nails through the sides to hold the mounting cleat in place. (See the top photo at right.) Then strengthen each joint with a couple of drywall screws. Next, fasten a countertop cleat to each case side, keeping the top face of the cleat flush with the top edge of the side.

7. Attach the back panel. Drive a few ⅝-in. brads to hold the panel in position. (See the bottom photo at right.) Then screw the panel to the case with ¾-in. screws. Drive several screws into the back edge of each case side, several screws into the mounting cleat, and several screws into the back edge of the bottom.

Building Corner Base Cabinets

Corner base cabinets are unique because they take up 36 in. of wall space on each side of the corner but are only 18 in. deep. (See the drawing on p. 92.) There are a couple of reasons for this size. First, a cabinet that is 36 in. square does not fit through a standard doorway. Second, when you use the measurements shown in the drawing on p. 92, the side and floor panels for two corner cases can be cut from one sheet of plywood. This corner case can accommodate a 24-in.-diameter lazy Susan.

Building a corner base cabinet is very much like building a standard base cabinet. Follow these steps:

1. Assemble the base frame. Dimensions for the frame are shown in the drawing on p. 92.

2. Attach the base frame to the floor panel with pocket screws.

I nail the mounting cleat between the side panels at the back of the cabinet, then strengthen each joint with a couple of 1⅝-in. screws.

Nailing on the back panel finishes the construction of the base cabinet.

PRO TIP

Plate-joinery biscuits can swell from moisture, making them fit too tightly. Shrink swollen biscuits by putting them in a microwave oven for a minute or two.

TRADE SECRET

Assembling cases is faster and easier when you have an air-powered finish nailer. This tool enables you to hold two parts in exact alignment with one hand, then "tack" the joint together with a couple of well-placed air-driven nails. The tacked connection will hold the assembly until you can fasten it securely with screws.

Corner Cabinet Bracing

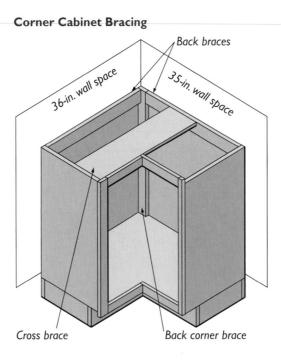

Back braces

36-in. wall space

35-in. wall space

Cross brace

Back corner brace

3. Install the side panels. Drive a few nails to hold each panel in place until you can secure each side-to-floor joint with 2-in. screws.

4. Install the bracing material at the back of the case. These braces, which I usually cut from ¾-in. plywood, provide a nailing surface for attaching the back. (See the center photo on the facing page.)

5. Attach the face frame. If you haven't done so already, assemble the right-angled frame before attaching it to the front of the case. As with a standard base cabinet, the face frame is attached with pocket screws driven through holes in the case sides. (See the bottom left photo on the facing page.) For strength and alignment, I use biscuit joints where the frame's bottom rails meet the front edge of the bottom panel.

Corner Cabinet Case—Exploded View

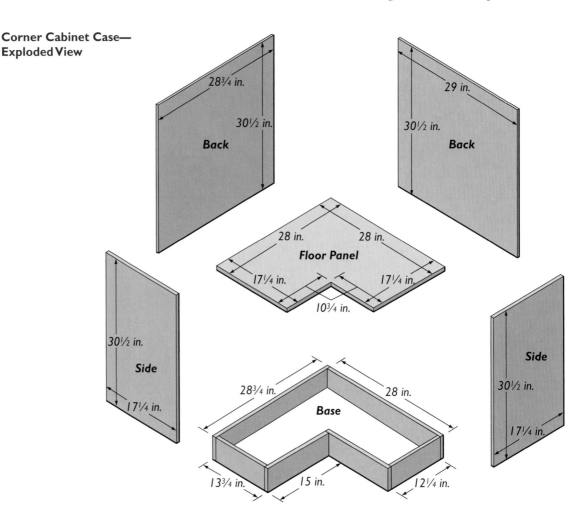

28¾ in.

30½ in.

Back

29 in.

30½ in.

Back

28 in.　28 in.

Floor Panel

17¼ in.　17¼ in.

10¾ in.

30½ in.

Side

17¼ in.

28¾ in.　28 in.

Base

13¾ in.　15 in.　12¼ in.

Side

30½ in.

17¼ in.

The corner cabinet's base frame is an L-shaped assembly made from six pieces of ³/₄-in. plywood.

A couple of finishing nails will hold the side panel in place until the joint can be reinforced with screws.

Brace the back of the corner case with ³/₄-in.-thick, 2-in.-wide wood cleats. These braces provide a nailing surface for attaching the back.

Use pocket screws to attach the corner cabinet's right-angled face frame to the sides of the case.

A cross brace extends across the top of the cabinet and is pocket-screwed to one of the face frame's top rails. Check for square, as shown, when installing the brace.

PRO TIP

When assembling a corner base cabinet, don't forget to install the lazy Susan hardware inside the case before attaching the back panels.

TRADE SECRET

Once a cabinet is complete, it's important to protect the edges and corners so they don't get bumped and damaged in transit or storage. Fold heavy cardboard to form a right-angled corner. Tack, staple, or tape the cardboard on the cabinet to protect vulnerable edges.

IN DETAIL

When building solid end panels with a 45-degree corner stile, cut the bottom plywood in a 45-degree angle. To find the correct distance, measure 2⁹/₁₆ in. from each corner, mark the distance, and draw a diagonal line across the two points. This is the cut line.

6. Install the cross brace. (See the bottom right photo on p. 93.) Make sure this brace is wide enough (at least 8 in. or so) to cross the center of the case where the lazy Susan's mounting collar will be secured. Check the top of the face frame for square before screwing the cross brace to one of the face-frame rails and to the sides of the case.

Building End Panel Cabinets

A base cabinet that will be exposed on one side needs to be built differently than an in-line cabinet. As shown in the photo at right, I like to incorporate a 45-degree corner in this type of cabinet, as well as a frame-and-panel assembly on the exposed side of the cabinet. These end panels look nice if they are built in the same style as the cabinet doors. For details on how to make frame-and-panel doors, end panels, and the decoratively fluted 45-degree corner, see Chapter 5. In this section, I will concentrate on how to incorporate the 45-degree corner into the base cabinet's construction.

1. Rabbet the back edge of the side panel. This will conceal the cabinet's ¼-in.-thick back panel. I cut the rabbet with a router and a rabbeting bit.

2. Fasten the corner board to the end panel. Before it's trimmed flush, the corner board measures 5⅛ in. wide, with 45-degree bevels cut along both long edges. (See the drawing on the facing page.) To join the board to the end panel, I use a simple jig that keeps the parts aligned as I drive the installation screws. (See the top right photo on the facing page.) This joint should also be glued.

3. Plane off the protruding bevel. After pulling the joint tight with pocket screws, flip

The side of a cabinet that will be visible after installation can receive special treatment. I like to build a frame-and-panel side and join it to the end cabinet's face frame with a 45-degree corner.

over the assembly so you can plane off the bevel that extends beyond the end panel. This takes just a few passes with a handplane, as shown in the center left photo on the facing page.

4. Join the face frame to the corner board. Use glue and screws to join the face-frame stile to the board. Spread glue on the mating parts, clamp together the joint, and drill counterbored pilot holes for the screws. (See the bottom photo on the facing page.) Once all the screws are driven and the joint is secure, fill the counterbored holes with dowel plugs, which can be cut and sanded flush after the glue dries. The beveled edge of the board will extend slightly beyond the face frame, just as it did along the end panel. Plane it flush as described previously.

5. Cut and install the case bottom. Lay out the 45-degree cut on the corner of the case bottom. As shown in the drawing on the facing page, this cut should be the diagonal of a 2⁹/₁₆-in. square. Make the cut with a handsaw, then assemble the case.

After constructing the end panel, I rout a rabbet on the back inside edge where the cabinet back will fit.

A jig aligns the angled joint between the end panel and the angled board while the pocket screws are driven.

With a handplane, remove the beveled corner that extends beyond the face of the panel.

Use a fine-tooth handsaw to trim off the 45-degree corner of the cabinet's bottom panel.

Adding a 45-Degree Corner

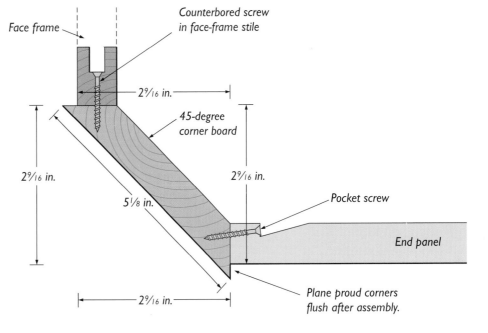

Face frame

Counterbored screw in face-frame stile

2⁹/₁₆ in.

45-degree corner board

2⁹/₁₆ in.

2⁹/₁₆ in.

5¹/₈ in.

Pocket screw

End panel

2⁹/₁₆ in.

Plane proud corners flush after assembly.

Glue and screw the cabinet's face frame to the angled board.

Wall Cabinets

CHAPTER EIGHT

1 Dimensions and Design Options, p. 98

2 Cutting and Joinery Details, p. 98

3 Assembling Standard Wall Cabinets, p. 101

4 Building End Panel Cabinets, p. 103

5 Building Corner Wall Cabinets, p. 104

When you look at wall cabinets, what you notice are the doors, not the cases. But beautifully made doors deserve solid, accurately made cases. In this chapter, we'll cover case construction for three types of wall cabinets. A standard wall cabinet can be sized to hold a single door, double doors, or even two sets of doors, one above the other.

An end panel cabinet has one side exposed after the cabinet is installed, so this side needs special treatment. As with end panel base cabinets, I usually build a frame-and-panel side instead of a plywood side. This solid wood panel can join the face frame at either a 90-or 45-degree angle.

The third type of wall cabinet is designed to fit in a corner. It has a single door and is usually kept open inside so that a lazy Susan can be installed.

PRO TIP

When labeling parts, mark the back or an unseen side of a piece so you won't have to sand off the writing later.

IN DETAIL

When a woodworker says that a joint meets at a 45-degree angle, the actual angle could be 90 degrees plus 45 degrees, or 135 degrees. Likewise, a bevel cut of 67½ degrees may be referred to as 22½ degrees (90 degrees minus 67½ degrees). Woodworkers typically refer to the lesser angle because they're thinking about how the blade will be tilted on the table saw or chopsaw to make the cut. By subtracting 90 degrees from the actual measurement of the angle, you obtain the proper tilt angle for the blade.

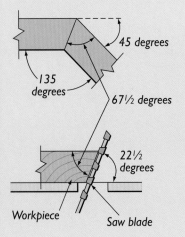

45 degrees

135 degrees

67½ degrees

22½ degrees

Workpiece

Saw blade

Dimensions and Design Options

Most wall cabinets are just 12 in. deep, including the face frame and the back of the cabinet. But unlike base cabinets, which have a standard height, wall cabinets can be as tall or as short as space allows. You can make cabinets tall enough to extend all the way to the ceiling, but the additional storage space this creates can't be reached without a step stool. In a kitchen with an 8-ft. ceiling, 30-in.-tall cabinets are often used, and 42-in.-tall cabinets look good with a 9-ft. ceiling.

The bottom of the cabinet can be flush with the bottom of the cabinet's sides and face frame. But I prefer to recess the bottom panel so its top surface is flush with the top edge of the face frame's bottom rail. (See the drawing on the facing page.) This makes the inside of the cabinet easy to clean and more attractive when cabinet doors are open. Another advantage is the recess allows you to install concealed under-cabinet lighting.

As shown in the drawing above, there are several types of wall cabinets. Whenever possible, I try to build a double-door cabinet instead of joining smaller single-door units. It's important to size your cabinets so you can handle them comfortably in the shop and during installation. The time to make these decisions is when you are building the face frames (see Chapter 4), since the dimensions of the frame determine the size of the cabinet case.

As with base cabinets, it's fine for screws, nails, and the back panel to show on the side of a finished wall cabinet, as long as the cabinet will be joined to another unit. When the side will be visible after the cabinet is installed, I build a solid wood end panel and install that instead of a plywood side. The back edge of the end panel needs to be rabbeted to hold and hide the cabinet back. See Chapter 5 for details on building end panels.

Types of Wall Cabinets

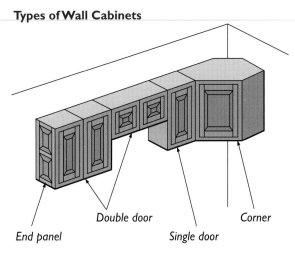

End panel Double door Single door Corner

Cutting and Joinery Details

Whether you're building one cabinet or many, it's good to make a cutlist so you can keep track of all the parts. This list also enables you to get the optimum number of parts from each sheet of plywood. Since cabinet cases can be assembled with butt joints, it's easy to calculate the sizes of different parts. Basic dimensions and joinery details are shown in the drawing on the facing page. The completed width of a standard cabinet case should be ½ in. less than the width of the face frame. This allows each outer stile to extend ¼ in. beyond the case side. When one side of the cabinet will be exposed, the face frame makes a flush joint (at either a 90- or a 45-degree angle) with the solid end panel, and no ¼-in. extension is used.

When cutting plywood parts to their finished sizes, try to take advantage of one rip fence setting to cut all the parts that share the same width. This ensures duplicate sizes. For most of the wall cabinets that I build, the plywood side panels for cases are 11 in. wide. But the bottom and top panels share this 11-in. width, too. Make sure you label the parts as you cut them, as the sides, tops, and bottoms may be similarly sized.

Wall Cabinet—Construction Overview

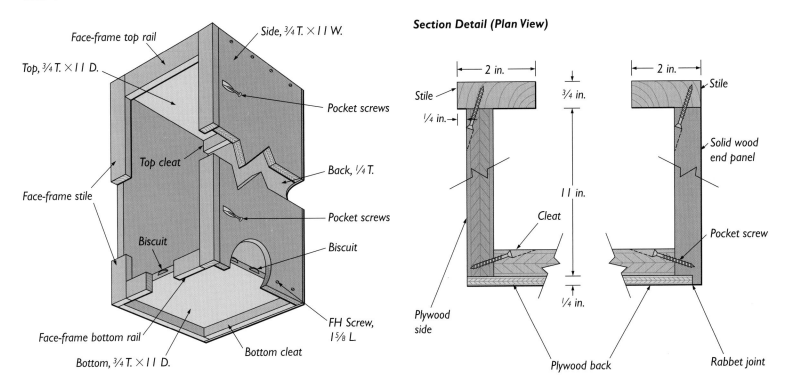

- Face-frame top rail
- Side, ¾ T. × 11 W.
- Top, ¾ T. × 11 D.
- Pocket screws
- Top cleat
- Back, ¼ T.
- Face-frame stile
- Pocket screws
- Biscuit
- Biscuit
- FH Screw, 1⅝ L.
- Face-frame bottom rail
- Bottom cleat
- Bottom, ¾ T. × 11 D.

Section Detail (Plan View)

- 2 in.
- Stile
- ¾ in.
- ¼ in.
- 11 in.
- Stile
- Solid wood end panel
- Cleat
- Pocket screw
- ¼ in.
- Plywood side
- Plywood back
- Rabbet joint

Pocket holes and biscuit slots

After cutting all the plywood panels to size, I do the joinery work required to assemble the cases. As shown in the drawing above, the face frame is attached to the case top and sides with pocket screws. Using my pocket-hole jig, I bore these holes on the outside face of the panels, spacing them about 8 in. apart.

To join the bottom of the case to the sides, I use biscuit joints reinforced with screws. I use either four #10 biscuits or three #20 biscuits. If you want to recess the bottom panel, as I do, cut a strip of wood to use as a marking gauge for clamping a temporary fence to the side. (See the top photo on p. 99.) This marking gauge should be exactly as wide as the bottom rail of the face frame, which is 2 in. on most of the cabinets that I build. Clamp a temporary fence in place across the panel at the 2-in. line and mark the location of

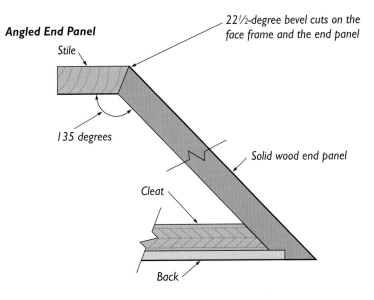

Angled End Panel

- 22½-degree bevel cuts on the face frame and the end panel
- Stile
- 135 degrees
- Solid wood end panel
- Cleat
- Back

TRADE SECRET

Shelf-support holes can be bored quickly and accurately in cabinet sides with a simple jig of evenly spaced holes. Store-bought drilling jigs are available, or you can make your own from pegboard paneling with ¼-in.-dia. holes. Use a depth stop when drilling holes to avoid going too deep.

Clamped across the case side, a fence guides the base of the biscuit joiner as I cut slots for attaching the bottom panel.

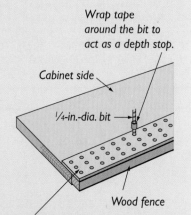

Wrap tape around the bit to act as a depth stop.

Cabinet side

¼-in.-dia. bit

Wood fence

Pegboard with ¼-in.-dia. holes

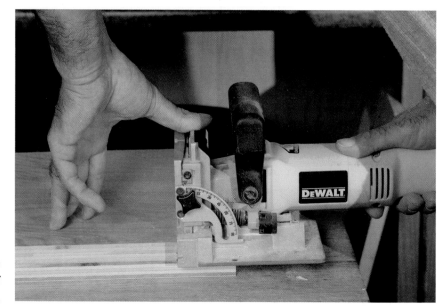

Matching slots are cut in the edge of the bottom panel.

the biscuit slots on the side and bottom panels. Now rest the base of the biscuit joiner against the temporary fence to cut the slots. With some biscuit-joiner models, you may need to remove the tool's fence first. Next, cut the corresponding biscuit slots in the edge of the bottom panel, as shown in the bottom photo above. Finish the biscuit-joinery work by cutting slots for the top of the case. Since the top will fit flush with the top

edges of the sides, you can use the biscuit joiner's fence to align these slots.

Shelf supports

On cabinets with glass doors, I usually install fixed shelves, keeping them in line with the horizontal mullions. But all other wall cabinets get adjustable shelves, so now is the time to either bore holes for shelf supports or dado the sides to accept shelving

Biscuits keep the joint aligned while you attach the bottom of the case to the side.

standards. A simple jig makes it easy to bore parallel rows of shelf-support holes. (See the Trade Secret on the facing page.) For more details on shelf supports, see Chapter 12.

Assembling Standard Wall Cabinets

The biscuits keep the joints aligned as you assemble the case. (See the photo above.) I apply glue in the biscuit slots, then join the sides, top, and bottom panels. (See the sidebar on p. 103.) With the case clamped square, I reinforce each panel joint with several 2-in. drywall screws. Then I attach the top and bottom cleats. (See the photo at right.) The cleats are important because you will fasten through them and into the wall when installing the cabinet. You can cut cleats from ply-

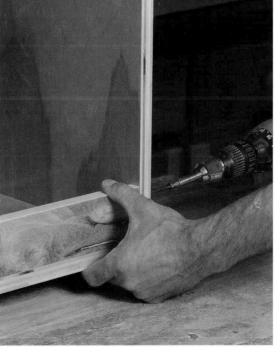

Attach the top and bottom cleats after assembling the case sides, top, and bottom.

PRO TIP

PRO TIP

When building a corner wall cabinet, don't forget to install the lazy Susan as you assemble the cabinet. (See Chapter 12 for details.)

TRADE SECRET

Cut from scrap wood, clamping blocks can help hold joints square during cabinet assembly. You can make these blocks in any size and at any angle. Use a jigsaw or a large-diameter hole saw (chucked in an electric drill) to bore holes for attaching spring clamps.

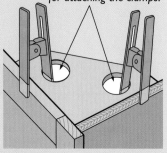

Bore holes in the brace for attaching the clamps.

WHAT CAN GO WRONG

When attaching face frames to cabinets with pocket screws, it's important to use the right clutch setting on your cordless drill. If the clutch is set too high, or if you have mistakenly switched from a clutch setting to "drill," it's easy to drive a pocket screw through the front of your face frame. To find the right clutch setting, experiment on some trial joints made from scrap wood.

Use biscuit slots on the front edge of the bottom panel to help attach the face frame.

Biscuit joints align the top edge of the face frame's bottom rail with the bottom of the cabinet's interior.

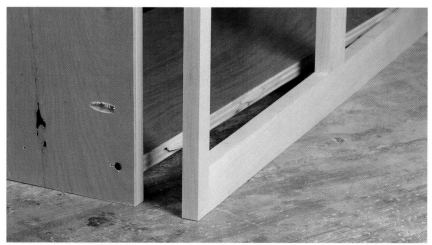

Tack the back in place with several brads, then secure it with ¾-in. screws.

wood or solid wood; I usually make them from plywood. If you want to hide the plywood edge, cover it with wood edgebanding before installing the cleat.

Install the face frame next. The biscuits align the bottom rail with the bottom of the cabinet, as shown in the photos above. The back is the last part to install. Even though the back is just ¼ in. thick, it adds rigidity to the case, keeping it square. For this reason, make sure the back panel is a true rectangle. Check it with a framing square. After tacking the back in place with several brads, screw it down with ¾-in. screws. (See the photo at left.)

A solid wood end panel looks much nicer than a plywood side. This one meets the cabinet's face frame at a 45-degree angle.

Building End Panel Cabinets

If one side of a wall cabinet will be exposed after installation, I replace this plywood side with one made from solid wood—usually a frame-and-panel assembly, as described in Chapter 5. This end panel can meet the face frame at a right angle, as with a standard cabinet. But if there's room in the kitchen, I like the look of an end panel that joins the face frame at a 45-degree angle, as shown in the photo above. If you want this type of end panel, both outside stiles will need to be bevel-cut.

To hide the ¼-in. plywood back, rabbet the back edge of the end panel, as shown in the drawing on p. 99. Use biscuit joints to attach the end panel to the top and bottom. Since you won't be able to drive screws into the "show" side of the panel to secure the joints, you'll need to clamp the cabinet together until the glue dries. I use pocket screws to attach the face frame to an end panel. These screws work whether the end panel joins the face frame at a 90- or 45-degree angle.

Advice to Stick With

Glue can provide just as much holding power as screws, so it definitely contributes to the overall sturdiness of your cabinets. But it can cause problems, too. Here's how to avoid them.

- **Don't apply too much.** When biscuit joints are used to join panels or face frames, it's not necessary to apply glue along the full length of the joint. Instead, simply spread glue in the biscuit slots. A small brush does a good job of coating the slot.

- **Remove squeeze-out carefully in "show" areas.** Using a damp rag to wipe off excess glue can actually spread glue deep into the surrounding wood. When that happens, you're sure to get a blotchy finish unless the affected area is thoroughly sanded. A better strategy is to let the squeeze-out dry to a rubbery consistency, then simply peel it off with a chisel or scraper. Alternatively, you can let the glue harden and then carefully chisel or scrape it off.

- **Beware of sticky fingers.** A finger is a fine glue-spreading tool, but you don't want to leave glue marks on every cabinet surface you touch. Tuck a damp rag into your back pocket so you can wipe your fingers clean.

TRADE SECRET

Wall cabinets deserve some special sanding treatment after they've been assembled. It won't take long, and it will make a difference in the quality of your finished installation. The first area to check out is the inside bottom surface of the cabinet. Make sure the top edge of the face frame's bottom rail is flush with the inside bottom of the cabinet. If you detect a slight ridge, sand it flush with 120-grit sandpaper to make the bottom easier to clean and use. Once you're done in that area, smooth any sharp inside corners of the face frame. This will make your cabinet a little more friendly to hands that happen to brush against the face frame.

Building Corner Wall Cabinets

Corner wall cabinets are built differently than corner base cabinets. Usually, I build this type of cabinet with a front that meets the adjoining wall cabinets at a 45-degree angle. (The angle formed actually measures 135 degrees, or 90 degrees + 45 degrees.) With more depth and a fairly wide door, this cabinet can accommodate a multiple-level lazy Susan, which makes the storage space inside the cabinet much more accessible.

Although the height of this cabinet can vary, other dimensions should stay the same. It is important to carefully dimension the parts so the cabinet can join neighboring cabinets correctly. As shown in the drawing below, this cabinet takes up 24 in. of wall space on each side of the corner. The back corner of the cabinet stops shy of the wall, thanks to an angled back support. This makes

it easier to install the cabinet, especially if the wall surfaces aren't square.

The front edge of each side panel is beveled at a 45 degree angle to meet the cabinet's face frame. The cleats and the back support also require 45-degree cuts. As shown in the detail drawing below, the stiles of the corner cabinet's face frame and the stiles of the adjoining cabinets are beveled 22½ degrees; when they are joined, they form a 135-degree angle (90 degrees + 45 degrees).

Cut the corner cabinet parts to the dimensions shown in the drawing on the facing page. The dimensions and angles in the top and bottom panels contain all the dimensions you need to cut the remaining parts. Once the parts are cut to size, you can cut the biscuit slots in the side, top, bottom, and face-frame bottom rail. Bore pocket holes in the sides to attach the face frame.

Now you're ready to assemble the case. You may need a few clamps to hold the panels together

Corner Wall Cabinets

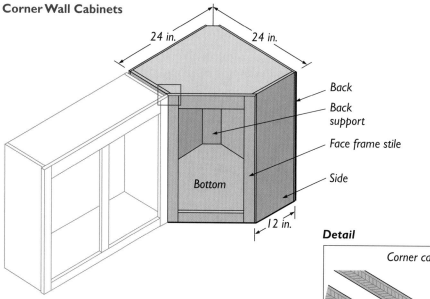

Corner wall cabinets take up 24 in. of wall space and measure 12 in. in depth to the outside edge of the face frame. For a smooth transition from the wall cabinet's face frames to the corner cabinet's face frame, the stiles of both face frames are mitered at a 22.5-degree angle.

Detail

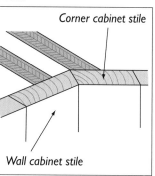

Screw the back support to the bottom of the corner cabinet.

until you can drive a few 2-in. screws to secure the joints. (See the Trade Secret on p. 102.)

Here's the assembly sequence I use. First, I join the side panels to the top and bottom. Then I install the back support, attaching it to the top and bottom with pocket screws (two per joint). Next I install the cleats, followed by the back panels, and finally the face frame. (See the photos above and below.)

Corner Cabinet Construction

Cabinet heights will vary, but other part dimensions remain fixed. Use the dimensions and angles in the top and bottom panels to size all remaining parts. All parts except for the 1/4-in.-thick back panels are 3/4 in. thick. The top cleats should be at least 2 in. wide.

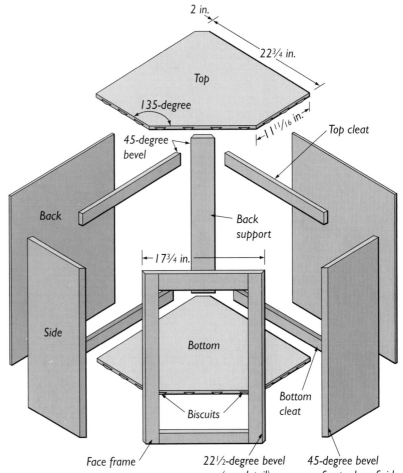

In a corner cabinet, each top cleat has a 45-degree bevel cut on the end that butts against the back support.

Other Cabinets

CHAPTER NINE

1 Wall Cabinets above the Stove, p. 108

A cabinetmaker's ability to do custom work truly comes into play when nonstandard cabinets need to be built. This chapter covers the main types of "other" cabinets that go into a kitchen. In many situations, these cabinets do not have standard measurements. Instead, they must be designed to accommodate built-in appliances or serve specific needs.

When a kitchen is filled with factory-made cabinets, it's often easy to tell that compromises have been made so that standard cases and face frames can be used. When you design and build your own cabinets, this "other" category offers an opportunity to add some distinctive craftsmanship while also enhancing the convenience of the kitchen.

2 Refrigerator Cabinets, p. 108

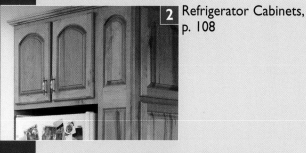

3 Cabinets for Wall Ovens, p. 109

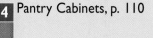

4 Pantry Cabinets, p. 110

5 Island Cabinets, p. 110

PRO TIP

It's tempting to build one large cabinet instead of two small ones. Just make sure the cabinet will fit through doors and hallways.

IN DETAIL

Here's how to calculate the overall height of pantry and other tall cabinets that extend to the top of adjacent wall cabinets:
Planned height of countertop (typically 36 in.),
plus
Planned distance between countertop and wall cabinets (18 in.),
plus
Finished height of adjacent wall cabinet (30 in.)
equals
Finished height of tall cabinet (usually 84 in.).

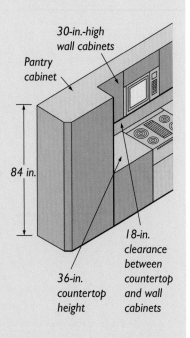

30-in.-high wall cabinets

Pantry cabinet

84 in.

18-in. clearance between countertop and wall cabinets

36-in. countertop height

Wall Cabinets above the Stove

This type of cabinet is usually a short case with two doors. (See the photo below.) It has the same 12-in. depth as standard wall cabinets, and its top is level with the tops of adjacent wall cabinets. But its width and height usually depend on the dimensions of the range hood or built-in microwave oven that will be installed directly above the stove.

These days, it's very popular to install a microwave oven above the stove. Available from numerous manufacturers, this built-in appliance is equipped with a ventilation fan and grease filter to exhaust hot air and odors from the stovetop. Ideally, the width of the microwave unit should match the width of the stove, which is usually 30 in.

Whether you are installing a venting microwave oven or just a vent hood, it's best to have the unit on hand before you build the wall cabinet that will fit above it. Use the manufacturer's instructions regarding the cabinet width and clearance above the stove. If the hood or microwave oven will be vented to the outside (more desirable than a recirculating vent), you'll need to run the ventilation ductwork prior to installing the cabinet. Wiring will also need to come through the back of the cabinet to power the vent fan and the microwave.

Refrigerator Cabinets

In its simplest form, a refrigerator cabinet is just a short wall cabinet sized to fit over the refrigerator. But I usually suggest that homeowners make this cabinet 24 in. deep. This puts the cabinet doors closer to the refrigerator door, adding more storage space and making the area at the front of the cabinet much more accessible. (See the left photo on the facing page.)

Single-door refrigerators are usually 30 in. wide, while most double-door models are 36 in. wide. As in other situations where cabinets are built around appliances, make sure the clearances match or exceed the appliance manufacturer's recommendations. A fit that's too tight for the refrigerator not only makes installation and replacement difficult, but it can also cause the unit to function poorly or fail prematurely.

Many kitchen layouts place the refrigerator at the end of a run of cabinets. If that is the case, I

Shorter than neighboring cases and fitted with double doors, an over-the-stove cabinet must match the width of the built-in microwave or vent hood installed below it.

A pantry cabinet extends to the full height of the wall cabinets and can be any depth you want. The cabinet over the refrigerator is deeper than a normal wall cabinet so contents are more accessible.

A full-height, full-depth cabinet is usually what you need for a built-in oven. This cabinet has solid wood side panels, a large lower drawer beneath the oven, and two tiers of cabinets above.

like to construct a full-height frame-and-panel end. The top of this assembly becomes the side of the wall cabinet above the refrigerator. This way, both sides of the appliance are concealed by custom cabinetwork that is much more attractive than painted steel.

Cabinets for Wall Ovens

If a kitchen design includes a wall-mounted oven, then a wall-oven cabinet will need to be integrated into the overall cabinetry plan. An oven cabinet is typically a tall case sized to house a single or double oven. (See the right photo above.) Depending on the overall layout of the kitchen, an oven cabinet can have standard base and wall cabinets on each side or on one side only.

Built-in ovens come in several standard widths; 24 in., 27 in., and 30 in. are the most common. The oven manufacturer's specifications will provide all the key measurements for designing a cabinet to house the unit. Make sure you adhere to these requirements when sizing cabinet parts. The dimension you can control is the vertical height of the oven unit. When I build these cabinets, I consider the heights of the users and sometimes adjust the height recommendations provided by the manufacturer. Above the oven, I normally extend the top of the cabinet to the same height as other wall cabinets or up to the kitchen's ceiling or soffit. But unlike a standard wall cabinet, which is just 12 in. deep, this upper cabinet is usually 24 in. deep.

When the sides of an oven cabinet will be visible in the finished installation, I make them as frame-and-panel assemblies. For instructions on

IN DETAIL

If the wall cabinets will fit against the ceiling, so the tall cabinets should, too. But you can't build a tall cabinet as high as the ceiling because it will be too tall to tip into place. A full-height cabinet that will be installed in a kitchen with a 96-in.-high ceiling should be no more than 92 in. high. To figure out how tall to make a full-height cabinet, use the following formula:

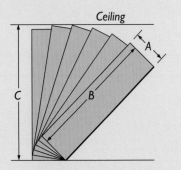

A = Finished width of cabinet
B = Maximum finished height
     of cabinet
C = Ceiling height

$$B = \left(\sqrt{C^2 - A^2}\right) - \tfrac{1}{4} \text{ in.}$$

making frame-and-panel sides and end panels, see Chapter 5.

Pantry Cabinets

In a typical kitchen, the pantry cabinet is usually the largest case built as a single unit. This type of cabinet can rest on a kickspace base, just like a standard base cabinet does. Alternatively, the front of the cabinet can extend all the way to the floor.

A pantry cabinet typically extends all the way to the ceiling, the soffit, or the top of the wall cabinets. In many kitchens, a pantry cabinet is located on one side of the refrigerator or at the end of a run of base and wall cabinets. This cabinet's main purpose is to keep packaged food organized and accessible.

When the cabinet is 24 in. deep, it's best to fit the interior with pull out shelves. In a shallower pantry cabinet, I install adjustable shelves. Build this type of cabinet just as you would a base cabinet. Cabinet sides that will be exposed after installation can be frame-and-panel assemblies instead

of plywood. (See Chapter 5.) Design the side panels so they are consistent with the appearance of the doors and drawer fronts on other cabinets.

Island Cabinets

The size of the average kitchen continues to grow. Open-plan kitchens and designs that accommodate more than one chef are popular. The kitchen island is an important element in this trend. Many islands incorporate broad countertops that overhang a row of stools or high chairs, creating a breakfast bar. Other islands are designed to include a sink, stovetop, or dishwasher.

The cabinets for an island usually need to be wider than a standard base cabinet and finished off nicely on all sides. Most islands are too large to be built as a single unit, so they need to be assembled from a series of cabinets. (See the sidebar on the facing page.) I usually build side, end, and back panels as frame-and-panel assemblies, using the tools and techniques described in Chapter 5.

When building island cabinetry, finish off all sides of the case. Here, a countertop overhangs a hickory cabinet to create a breakfast bar.

BUILDING A BIG ISLAND

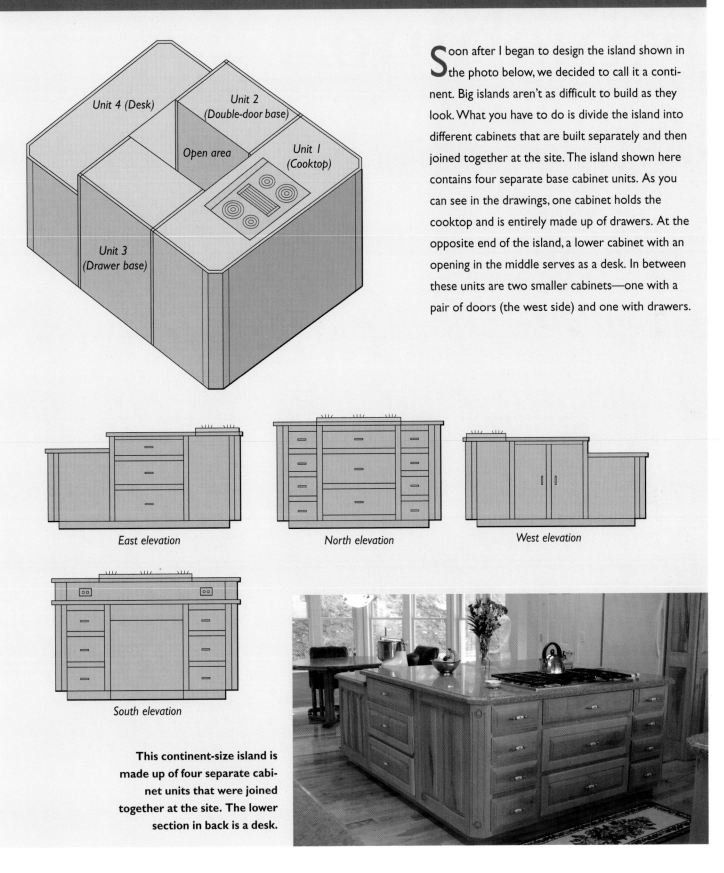

Unit 4 (Desk)

Unit 2 (Double-door base)

Open area

Unit 1 (Cooktop)

Unit 3 (Drawer base)

East elevation

North elevation

West elevation

South elevation

Soon after I began to design the island shown in the photo below, we decided to call it a continent. Big islands aren't as difficult to build as they look. What you have to do is divide the island into different cabinets that are built separately and then joined together at the site. The island shown here contains four separate base cabinet units. As you can see in the drawings, one cabinet holds the cooktop and is entirely made up of drawers. At the opposite end of the island, a lower cabinet with an opening in the middle serves as a desk. In between these units are two smaller cabinets—one with a pair of doors (the west side) and one with drawers.

This continent-size island is made up of four separate cabinet units that were joined together at the site. The lower section in back is a desk.

Finishing

CHAPTER TEN

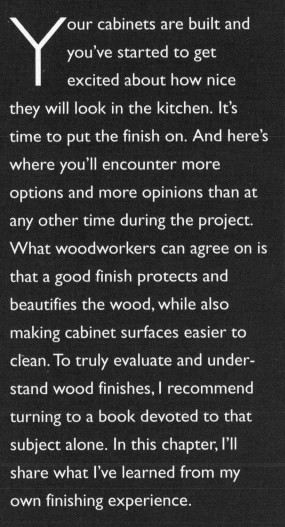

Your cabinets are built and you've started to get excited about how nice they will look in the kitchen. It's time to put the finish on. And here's where you'll encounter more options and more opinions than at any other time during the project. What woodworkers can agree on is that a good finish protects and beautifies the wood, while also making cabinet surfaces easier to clean. To truly evaluate and understand wood finishes, I recommend turning to a book devoted to that subject alone. In this chapter, I'll share what I've learned from my own finishing experience.

1 Sanding and Surface Preparation, p. 114

2 Choosing a Finish, p. 115

3 Using Paint and Stain, p. 121

PRO TIP

Before buying and using finish, make sure you read the label. To finish safely and successfully, follow the manufacturer's recommendations.

TRADE SECRET

The sticky surface of a tack cloth does an excellent job of removing sawdust from wood—the final step before you apply finish. You can buy a tack cloth where finishes are sold, or make your own by working a small amount of oil-based (alkyd) varnish into some cheesecloth. To maintain tackiness, fold the cloth over on itself and seal it in an airtight container.

WHAT CAN GO WRONG

Dust can ruin a finish, even in a workshop that appears completely clean. Commercial cabinet shops have dust-free finishing rooms, but many cabinet-makers don't have the luxury of a separate finishing room. Although it's possible to apply finish outdoors, insects can become trapped in varnish and other film-forming finishes. A better strategy is to clean your workshop as thoroughly as possible the day before applying finish. This gives airborne dust a chance to settle. Wipe each workpiece clean with a tack cloth. Choose a finish that either dries quickly (lacquer or fast-drying varnish, for example) or remains in the wood rather than on it (oil finish).

Sanding and Surface Preparation

Preparing wood for finishing is just as important as applying the finish—sometimes even more important. Make sure wood surfaces are smooth, clean, and free of dust before applying any finish. At this point, you should carefully inspect all the parts you are working on and repair any flaws. Fill cracks with filler or wood putty, and sand the filler flush once it dries. If any wood has been dented by a sharp impact, don't fill the depression before you try steaming out the dent, as described in the sidebar below.

Try to be smart about sanding. It's easy to waste time by oversanding. But it's also possible to sand too little; in that case, serious flaws will be highlighted by the finish. For example, there's no need to sand the back of a door with 400-grit sandpaper. Film finishes, such as lacquer and polyurethane, do not need a super-smooth surface to start. You can step up to a finer grit sandpaper when sanding between coats. Oil finishes, on the other hand, do require a smooth wood surface. I usually sand "show" surfaces (the fronts of doors and drawers) to 400 grit before applying oil.

Never sand across the grain unless you're smoothing the edge of a board and can't avoid it, and always hand-sand with the grain after using a random-orbit sander. Even the finest abrasives on a random-orbit sander leave swirl marks. To sand contoured areas—around doors and drawer fronts, for example—wrap sandpaper around a sponge, or buy sanding sponges in different grits. (See the photo below.)

Once you have finished sanding, vacuum as much sawdust as possible from your cabinet parts and your workspace. Avoid blowing sawdust with compressed air because this just stirs up lots of dust. Then wipe down all parts to be finished with a tack rag. You can buy these sticky rags where finishes are sold, or make your own. (See the Trade Secret at left.)

Smooth contoured areas with a store-bought sanding sponge, or make your own by wrapping sandpaper around a sponge.

Steaming out Dents

Wood that has been dented can often be repaired with steam, which causes compressed wood fibers to swell back to normal size. Dampen the dented area slightly, place a clean, damp rag over the dent, and go over the towel with a hot iron, applying light pressure only. Allow the wood to dry thoroughly, then sand the wood smooth.

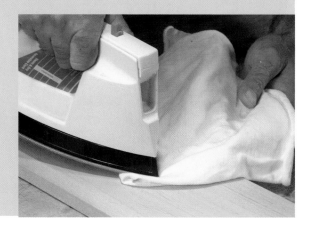

Choosing a Finish

If you talk to woodworkers and finishing experts, you'll hear many different opinions about wood finishes. And there certainly are many finishing products available. But just about everyone will agree that there's no such thing as the perfect finish. As you'll see in the descriptions that follow, some finishes are very durable, while others are easy to renew. Some finishes are tricky to apply or require special equipment; other finishes can be brushed or wiped on right in your workshop.

Whatever finish you choose, it should have some degree of scratch resistance and be able to seal the wood so stains and moisture can't penetrate. As you evaluate your finishing options, aim

The tremendous variety of finishes available today can make it difficult to choose the right product for your project. (Photo courtesy Lowe's Home Improvement Store, Franklin, NC.)

Finishing Safely

Don't risk your health when applying finish. Good ventilation is essential, even when you are using water-based finishes. In a garage or other workshop setting, you can open windows and use a fan to create good ventilation. Make sure the fan blows fresh air toward the finishing area and toward an open window in an exterior wall. Don't set up a fan to pull finish-laden air toward itself.

Read the safety instructions on the product, and always follow the manufacturer's recommenda-tions for ventilation and safe use. Conversion var-nish and lacquer are among the most dangerous finishes in terms of toxic fumes. When using those products, always wear an organic vapor respirator and have plenty of ventilation. Store filter car-tridges for organic vapor respirators in airtight containers when they're not in use. These car-tridges will degrade gradually when exposed to open air. If you smell the finish through the respi-rator, replace the cartridge immediately.

Good Ventilation for Finishing

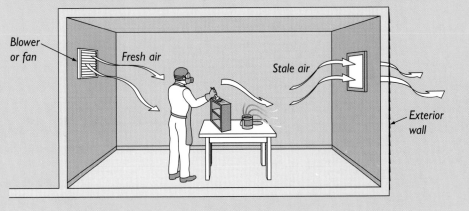

Blower or fan

Fresh air

Stale air

Exterior wall

TRADE SECRET

To significantly reduce the amount of airborne dust in your workshop, consider buying an air cleaner. Major tool manufacturers, such as Delta® and Jet®, sell air cleaners sized for small workshops. These machines draw air through a series of filters, trapping the dust particles that can harm your lungs and mar a finish.

WHAT CAN GO WRONG

Drips, runs, and sags can easily occur when a film-forming finish (varnish, lacquer, or shellac) is applied by brush or sprayed on to a vertical surface. If these finish defects are allowed to dry, they're unsightly and troublesome to remove. A good way to avoid drips, runs, and sags is to apply finish on a horizontal surface. Try to position cabinet doors, drawer fronts, and face frames horizontally before applying finish. Following application, inspect the lower edges of the workpiece and wipe smooth any drips and excess finish that you find.

for a treatment you can apply successfully and safely.

No matter which type of finish you choose, several preparation and application rules are universal. First, you need a clean, dust-free area for finishing. This is more important with some finishes than with others. Second, surface preparation is important. Sanding strategies and other surface prep steps will be covered later in this chapter. Finally, it's critical for wood to be finished equally on all sides. If you apply more coats on the outside of a door panel than on the inside, the inside surface will absorb more moisture, and that almost always leads to warping.

Conversion varnish

This is the standard finish used by cabinet manufacturers, who apply it with spray equipment. A mixture of alkyd resin and melamine resin (the hard resin used to make plastic laminates), conversion varnish provides the best resistance to stains, scratches, and moisture. Although it's the toughest finish for cabinetry, conversion varnish isn't used by many small-shop cabinetmakers because it can

be difficult to apply. A catalyst must be added to the finish just before application, and proper mixing is critical. Temperature and relative humidity must be controlled to achieve the best results, and the finish is almost impossible to repair. Health concerns also scare people away from conversion varnish. The finish emits toxic fumes during application and as it dries, so a commercial spray booth setup is necessary for safe application.

Nitrocellulose lacquer

Applied with spray equipment, this finish has been used for decades by many commercial cabinet manufacturers, as well as by small-shop professionals and amateur woodworkers. When applied with the proper equipment and in the right environment, nitrocellulose lacquer is hard to beat as a finish. For more details on spray-finishing, see the sidebar on the facing page.

Lacquer is fairly inexpensive and easy to use. The standard procedure is to build a durable finish by applying several thin coats. (See the photo below.) Thanks to lacquer's fast-drying character-

Applied with spray equipment, lacquer goes on in thin coats that dry quickly, enabling you to build up a multiple-coat finish in a single day.

istics, it's often possible to completely finish a full set of cabinets in a single day. Unlike conversion varnish, lacquer is easy to repair. But this finish also emits toxic fumes, so it's critical to wear an approved respirator and provide safe ventilation when applying it. A spray booth is not necessary but helpful for this finish.

Brushing lacquer

I prefer brushing lacquer to varnish because it dries faster but looks about the same and is nearly as durable. Products such as Deft Clear Wood Finish® are readily available at hardware stores

Brushing lacquer is easy to apply, and it dries quickly. Shop-made T–supports are useful aids when finishing small parts like this drawer front.

Spray Finishing Options

If you are building cabinets and other woodworking projects on a regular basis, you'll probably want to invest in a spray-finishing system. Applying finish with a spray gun is much faster than applying it with brushes or rags. To do spray finishing right, you'll need three things: 1) the right equipment; 2) a well-ventilated, fairly dust-free workspace; and 3) practice.

In terms of equipment, most woodworkers find that high-volume low-pressure (HVLP) models are preferable to conventional spray guns. Although both types of guns look the same, HVLP models are designed to minimize overspray. You have more control in applying the finish, and there's less mess and wasted finish. The main disadvantage with these guns is that they demand greater air volume than most small, shop-size air compressors can deliver. If you are setting up for spray-finishing, make sure your compressor's capacity is sufficient for the gun you plan to use. Some manufacturers offer finishing systems that include a compressor, an air hose, and a spray gun. Buying a system usually saves you money, and

you can be sure that the compressor is matched to the gun.

Proficiency at spray-finishing comes with a little practice. Success depends not only on your ability to keep the gun moving so that the finish is applied evenly, but also on how you support the workpiece and what spray sequence you use. For example, setting up a turntable will enable you to finish cabinet cases and other larger assemblies quickly and easily.

TRADE SECRET

If you spray-finish your cabinet cases after installing drawer-slide hardware, protect the case-mounted slide mechanisms with duct tape. Left unprotected, this hardware can become damaged by finish that drips on tracks and ball bearings.

WHAT CAN GO WRONG

Don't feel bad if you discover a small gap or two after you've applied finish. This happens from time to time, even to the most accomplished cabinet-makers. At this stage, you don't want to apply wood filler, sand it smooth, and refinish the piece. Instead, fill the gap using a colored wax stick. These sticks are available in a variety of hues where finishes are sold. Rub the stick over the gap to fill it, then buff the area with a clean, soft cloth. That does it.

and home improvement centers. (See the top photo on p. 117.)

As its name suggests, brushing lacquer is made for brush application. It has good flow-out properties, so brush marks are not a problem. For best results, apply brushing lacquer with a good-quality, natural bristle brush. Some lacquer finishes are best applied over a sanding sealer, so make sure you read the recommendations on the label.

Sanding sealer is a fast-drying clear finish that does an excellent job of sealing the wood in preparation for subsequent finish coats. Like brushing lacquer, it usually dries to the touch in less than one hour. For most cabinet parts, three coats of lacquer are sufficient. In high moisture locations—sink base cabinets, for example—apply five coats.

When applying lacquer, varnish, and shellac finishes, expect to do some sanding between coats. (See the photo below.) The main purposes of between-coat sanding are to remove any unevenness in the coat and to scuff the finish so it has enough "tooth" for the next coat to adhere to.

After sanding, be sure to wipe the finished surface clean of dust before applying the next coat.

Polyurethane varnish

"Poly" has become a very popular finish because of its durability and water resistance. Oil-based and water-based versions of this varnish are available. Oil-based polyurethane tends to impart an amber tone to the wood, while most water-based polyurethanes are completely clear. For a dull or low-luster finish, choose satin poly. Semigloss and gloss versions are also available, but most people don't like a shiny finish on their cabinets.

Depending on the formulation that you buy, polyurethane varnish can be applied with a brush with spray equipment. If you are interested in a spray finish that doesn't pose a health hazard, look into water-based polyurethane. You'll also find gel versions of this finish, which can be applied with a rag.

The main disadvantage with polyurethane varnish is that it can be difficult to repair or recoat. Once the finish has cured, subsequent coats of

Surface finishes, such as lacquer and varnish, often require light sanding between coats. You can do this with extra-fine sandpaper or an abrasive pad.

Building a Drying Rack

A drying rack can streamline your finishing work simply by providing convenient storage space for just-finished cabinet parts. The rack I use for holding drawers, doors, and drawer fronts can be quickly built from 2×4s and ½-in. dowel rods. Bore enough holes in the 2×4 uprights so you can reposition the dowels as necessary. A close vertical spacing will enable you to hold a good number of doors. Reposition the dowels when you need room for holding deep drawers.

finish do not adhere well. To solve this problem, lightly sand the surface to scuff up the existing finish. Another problem you may encounter with some brands of polyurethane (especially oil-based ones) is an extended drying time. When a finish remains wet or tacky for hours after application, airborne dust can become trapped in it. For best results, select a poly finish that dries quickly. To store parts while the finish dries, build a drying rack like the one shown above.

Shellac

Shellac is one of the oldest clear finishes. Despite the improved durability of more modern finishes, shellac is still favored by traditional woodworkers.

Repairing an Oil Finish

Oil finishes and varnish/oil blends are easy to repair—during initial finishing, after cabinet installation, and even years after construction. If wax was applied over the finish, first remove it by wiping the wood surfaces with a rag dampened with mineral spirits. Sand out scratches, taking care to finish up with extra-fine (220- or 320-grit) abrasives. Wipe the wood clean, apply a light coat of finish, let it stand, then buff off the excess. If some areas show heavy wear, apply a second or third coat to improve durability.

TRADE SECRET

It can be difficult to achieve a smooth finish on coarse-grained, open-pored woods, such as oak, hickory, and ash. One way to achieve smoother results with an oil finish is to wet-sand the wood as you're applying the finish. First flood the wood surface with oil, then sand the finish with 400-grit wet-or-dry sandpaper. (See the photo above.) The sawdust you create mixes with the oil and is rubbed into the open pores of the wood. After 5 to 10 minutes, wipe off the extra oil/sawdust mixture and buff the surface smooth. The next day, lightly dry-sand the wood with 400-grit paper to remove any surface film, then continue the oil applications.

You can make your own wiping varnish by combining equal parts boiled linseed oil, alkyd varnish, and naphtha.

It's safe to use and made from natural ingredients—a resin that comes from insects. Although ready-made shellac is available, most woodworkers choose to make their finish as they need it by dissolving dried shellac flakes in alcohol solvent.

Shellac's fast drying time can make brush application tricky, especially when you have a broad surface to cover. Lap marks can be created where wet finish is brushed over dried finish. Better results are achieved when the finish is sprayed on. Shellac can be used as a finish on its own or as a sealer coat beneath varnish. It wipes clean easily but can be stained by standing water.

Oil finishes

Unlike polyurethane varnish and shellac, oil finishes aren't meant to form a protective film on the wood surface. Instead, this type of finish is applied generously and then wiped off. The remaining finish hardens in the pores of the wood, forming a barrier that repels water and resists staining, though not as effectively as varnish does. Some of these penetrating finishes are known as Danish oil or teak oil. Other folks

simply say "oil finish" to describe any finish that is flooded onto the wood and then wiped off.

Oil finishes are foolproof. Apply them generously, wipe off the excess, let the finish dry, then start over again. If your workshop is even moderately clean, you can apply a penetrating oil finish without worrying about dust contamination. Oil finishes are also the easiest to repair and maintain. (See the sidebar on p. 119.)

Shop-made oil-varnish finish

My favorite finish for cabinets is an oil-varnish blend that I mix up in my workshop. The oil penetrates and brings out the natural beauty of the wood, while the varnish provides extra protection. The formula I use is inexpensive and the ingredients are available wherever paints and finishes are sold. (See the photo above.) To duplicate this mixture, blend equal parts mineral spirit solvent, boiled linseed oil, and oil-based (alkyd) varnish. For a faster-drying finish, replace the mineral spirits with naptha. With experience, you'll learn to tailor this finish to different wood species. For example, you may want a thinner (greater solvent content) finish to go on tight-grained wood, such as maple.

The finish can be brushed, sprayed, or wiped on to the wood surface. I often apply the finish with an inexpensive disposable foam brush. (See the photo at right.) After applying it, let the finish soak into the wood for 10 to 15 minutes, then thoroughly wipe off the excess. The drying time is long—24 hours between coats. But since the wood is buffed clean between coats, dust deposits are not a problem. Varnish blends do not raise the grain of the wood, so the wood can be sanded to its final stage before applying the finish. A minimum of three coats will provide adequate protection.

Using Paint and Stain

Although I'm rarely asked to give cabinets a painted finish, this treatment does have its advantages. Paint covers unattractive wood grain and wood surfaces that have been marred by too much wood putty or filler. It also provides a very durable, easy-to-clean finish. If you are going to paint your cabinets, a semigloss paint is usually the best choice.

Stain allows the wood grain to show. There are colored stains that give wood a distinct hue—white, green, or yellow, for example. And there are stains designed to darken wood, usually to make it look older or like another wood species. I try to talk my customers out of staining wood, because popular species (cherry, maple, and pine, for example) do not stain well. Density changes in the same board cause stains to penetrate unevenly, creating blotches. To reduce blotchiness, I use a wood conditioner before staining. (See the photo at right.) Available where finishes are sold, wood conditioner is a clear sealer that helps stain penetrate evenly.

An inexpensive foam brush is fine for applying an oil finish. Flood the wood surface with finish, then wipe off the excess after 10 to 15 minutes.

Treating bare wood with a wood conditioner before applying finish can prevent uneven absorption, which causes a blotchy appearance.

Hardware

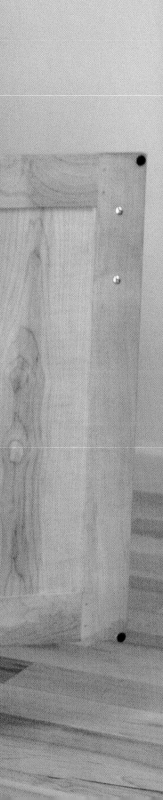

CHAPTER ELEVEN

There are many kinds of hardware used in kitchen cabinets. In this chapter, I'll cover just the essentials: hinges for cabinet doors, slide hardware for drawers, and knobs and pulls for drawers and doors. For other types of hardware, such as lazy Susan turntables, see Chapter 12.

When buying hardware, be wary of bargain-priced products. You usually get what you pay for. Cabinet doors and drawers receive heavy use every day, and good-quality components will outlast discount brands. Most hardware suppliers offer volume discounts, so you'll save some money by ordering enough units for a full kitchen.

1 Concealed Hinges, p. 124

2 Drawer-Slide Hardware, p. 128

3 Knobs and Pulls, p. 131

4 Attaching Drawer Fronts, p. 132

IN DETAIL

If you plan to install slide-out trays behind base cabinet doors, it's important to select and position the hinges correctly. The doors need to open fully, so choose hinges that open to 165 or 170 degrees. Also, make sure the hinges are located above or below tray level. In the photo below, for example, the lower door hinge is positioned above the lower tray.

Concealed Hinges

Euro hinges, also known as concealed or cup hinges, have become the most popular hinges for cabinet doors. Today, even inexpensive factory-made cabinets come with this type of hinge. Despite its complex-looking mechanism, a concealed hinge is not difficult to install if you have the right tools. The clip-on Euro hinges that I like to use allow you to remove and reattach a cabinet door quickly and easily. (See the photo below.) Another important benefit: Euro hinges are adjustable. Without removing the door or detaching the hinges, you can shift the door's position to keep it perfectly aligned.

I can think of only a couple of reasons to not use Euro hinges. You may want to use butt hinges if you are building cabinets with inset doors. But as explained in the sidebar on the facing page, Euro hinges can also be used on inset doors. If you are building lipped doors, inexpensive overlay hinges can be used instead of Euro hinges.

Make sure you select two-piece hinges. There is a hinge arm that includes a cup flanked by two flanges with holes for installation screws. A separate mounting plate completes the hinge. To install the hinge, bore a hole in the door where the cup will fit, using a 35mm or 1⅜-in. Forstner bit. You'll also need to drill a pair of pilot holes for two installation screws. The spacing for these holes can vary, depending on the manufacturer. The mounting plate is screwed to the stile of the face frame.

Whether you are ordering concealed hinges from a mail-order or an online source or buying them from a local supplier, use these specifications:

- **Opening angle:** 110 degrees for regular doors; 165 degrees for corner cabinets and standard cabinets fitted with pullout trays
- **Crank:** 0mm
- **Overlay:** Full
- **Style:** Clip-on
- **Mounting plate:** Face-frame mounting plate for ½-in. overlay.

Euro hinges come in two parts. The hinge arm is installed on the back of the door. It clips onto a mounting plate that's screwed to the face-frame stile.

Compile the hinge order for all your cabinets, and order in quantity to get the best price. The door for a base or wall cabinet requires just two hinges. For taller pantry doors, you may need three or four hinges. Manufacturers usually provide a maximum load rating to help you determine how many hinges are required for a pantry door.

Installing concealed hinges

Here are the four steps required to install concealed hinges.

1. Bore cup holes in the doors. It's important for each hole to be a uniform distance from the edge of the door—usually around ¼ in. Bore some trial holes in scrap material to determine the correct distance, then set up a fence on your drill press to align each hole. (See the top photo on p. 126.) You'll need to adjust the depth stop to match the depth of the cup. If you don't have a drill press, you can buy jigs designed for use with a portable electric drill. Available from mail-order suppliers, this type of jig aligns the cup hole and also provides depth adjustment.

Hardware for Inset Doors and Drawers

Although it's traditional to use butt hinges on cabinets with inset doors, you may want to consider using concealed Euro hinges instead. For one thing, Euro hinges are easier to install. They're also easy to adjust, enabling you to keep your doors hanging perfectly. Because of this adjustability, your doors can be installed with smaller clearances.

A Euro hinge for an inset door usually requires a 16mm crank and a zero-clearance face plate. Instead of being mounted on the face frame, Euro hinges are mounted on the face plate on the side of the cabinet. If the cabinet side isn't flush with the inside edge of the face frame, install a cleat inside the cabinet to create a flush mounting surface, as shown in the top photo at right.

Drawer-slide hardware for inset drawers is installed in much the same way as it is for overlay drawers. The main difference is that the front edge of the slide mechanism must be set back from the face frame, as shown in the bottom photo at right.

Euro hinges can be used on inset doors, but the mounting plate must be installed inside the cabinet instead of on the face frame.

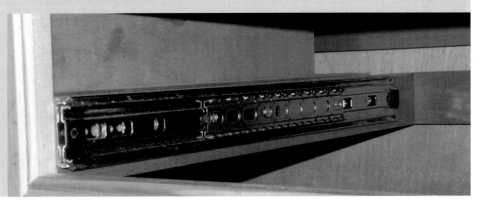

Drawer-slide hardware for an inset drawer should not extend onto the face frame.

PRO TIP

Store ball-bearing slide hardware so it won't get contaminated by workshop dust.

IN DETAIL

When using rear-mounting clips to install drawer slides, strengthen the back of the cabinet where the clips will be attached by gluing and screwing a ¾-in.-thick vertical cleat to the back panel.

IN DETAIL

Lazy Susan corner base cabinets have two doors attached to each other with special 90-degree inside corner hinges. The door attached to the case needs to be able to swing out of the way for easier access to the already-narrow opening. Hinges that open to at least 165 degrees are best suited for this purpose.

To install a Euro hinge, start by drilling a 35mm cup hole. Use a fence on the drill press to maintain a uniform distance from the edge of the door.

A small square keeps the hinge arm perpendicular to the door edge as you drill pilot holes for the installation screws. Use a Vix bit to make sure the holes are centered. (See the sidebar on the facing page.)

Where the cup hole is located relative to the top or bottom of the door is not that important, but it's best to establish a standard distance and stick with that. Just make sure the hinge locations don't interfere with the operation of pullout trays in base cabinets.

2. Screw the hinge arms to the doors. Fit the cup of the hinge arm in its hole. Then use a small square to hold the hinge arm at a right angle to the edge of the door while drilling pilot holes for the installation screws. (See the photo at left.) Use a self-centering Vix® bit to bore these holes. (See the sidebar on the facing page.) Make sure you don't drill through the "show" face of the door. Drive the installation screws after drilling the holes.

3. Attach the mounting plates to the face-frame stiles. A good way to position the mounting plates correctly is to attach them first to their hinge arms, and then hold the door in its installed position while screwing the plate to the stile. (See the bottom photo on the facing page.) To make it easier to hold the door accu-

Vix Bits Make Precision Easy

When mounting Euro hinges and other types of hardware that are installed with screws, it's very important to bore perfectly centered pilot holes. Vix bits are designed to do this quickly and easily. At first glance, these special bits don't look like bits at all. That's because the familiar twist drill bit remains hidden inside a spring-loaded outer mechanism until downward pressure is applied. The tapered tip of the bit's housing is designed to center the bit in holes bored in different types of hardware. To mount most types of cabinet hardware, buy a #3 and a #5 Vix bit. They cost about $10 apiece.

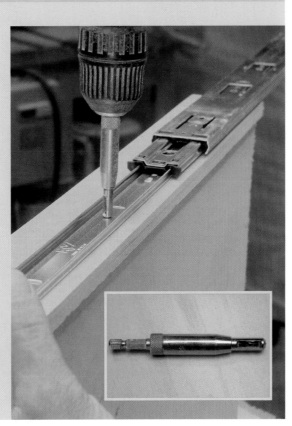

A Vix bit is designed to bore perfectly centered holes for hardware installation screws. The outer housing has a tapered tip to center a spring-loaded twist drill bit that extends when downward pressure is applied.

rately in place, I temporarily clamp a wood block against the face frame's bottom rail. This supports the bottom edge of the door.

4. Fine-tune the door's position. Once the mounting plates are attached, you can adjust the position of the door by loosening one or more screws, repositioning the door, then driving the screws tight.

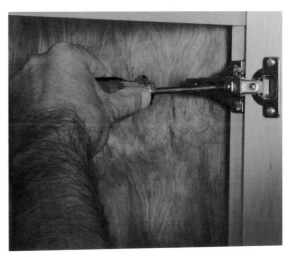

With the hinge arms and mounting plates clipped together and the door supported by a block of wood clamped to the cabinet, you can screw the mounting plates to the face frame.

PRO TIP

To distinguish between a knob and a pull, just remember that a knob is installed with a single screw. A pull requires two screws.

TRADE SECRET

Knobs and pulls can dramatically alter the overall appearance of your cabinet fronts. Take your time and select this hardware carefully. Also, remember that you have the option of doing without knobs and pulls. By routing a hollow or cove on the inside edges of doors and drawer fronts, you can create a fingerhold that eliminates the need for this hardware.

WHAT CAN GO WRONG

Ball-bearing drawer slides require a perfect fit for the best operation. When the drawer box fits too loosely in its opening, there's too much clearance for the slide mechanism to operate smoothly. You can improve this situation by inserting a small shim between where the back of the slide is attached to the face frame. (See the photo below.) It may also be necessary to shift the back of the slide slightly.

Side-mount slides are secured to the face frame and to the back of the cabinet. The slotted installation flanges compensate for a less-than-perfect fit.

Nylon roller slides operate smoothly and are less expensive than most other types of drawer slides.

Drawer-Slide Hardware

There are quite a few types of drawer-slide hardware. The least expensive drawer slides can sell for as little as $2.50 per pair, while top-of-the-line sets can go for $35 or more. The type you select for your kitchen cabinet doors depends on your budget and the overall appearance you want to achieve. The slide hardware used in kitchen base cabinets is usually 22 in. long and rated to support at least 100 lbs. You may want a greater load rating for large drawers.

Nylon roller slides are the most common slides used in manufactured cabinets. Inexpensive and easy to use, these slides are also the most forgiving when it comes to tolerances. (See the photo at left.) On the down side, drawers that run on these slides are usually limited to a three-quarter extension, and the slides allow a fair amount of racking when fully extended. Drawer boxes installed with nylon roller slides need to be 1 in. shallower and 1 in. narrower than the face-frame opening.

Side-mount ball-bearing slides are my favorite. This type of slide is a good compromise between sloppy nylon slides and expensive hidden slides. Ball-bearing slides can handle constant use, and it seems that the more load they carry, the smoother they operate. For a little more money you can buy over-travel slides that allow the back of the drawer to slide out beyond the front of the cabinet. (See the top photo on the facing page.) Of course,

With an over-travel slide, the back of the drawer can be pulled out beyond the face frame.

these and other side-mount slides are visible when the drawer is open, which can detract from the appearance of a dovetailed drawer. And side-mount slides require a ½-in. clearance space on each side of the drawer box. The fit needs to be just right for the slide to operate smoothly.

Under-mount or concealed drawer slides are the elite of drawer-slide hardware. These slides also run on ball bearings, so they're super smooth. They are installed in pairs, out of sight on the underside of the drawer box. Unfortunately, under-mount ball-bearing slides are the most expensive slides on the market; they're also very time-consuming to install. But if you want to show off a beautiful dovetailed drawer, this is the hardware to choose.

Installing drawer slides

Installing drawer slides can be a straightforward job or a frustrating, time-consuming task. It depends on your familiarity with the hardware and how accurately the boxes are sized. Each type of drawer slide discussed previously has two parts—one that's fastened to the cabinet and another that's screwed to the drawer box. You'll notice that there are round and slotted holes in each part. When you first secure each part, always

Screw the drawer half of the slide to the side of the drawer.

drive screws in the slotted holes. This will allow you to shift the slide's position slightly before driving the final installation screws.

The standard method for installing drawer-slide hardware is explained later and requires just three steps. I also use an alternate installation technique, explained in the sidebar on p. 130. Here are the three steps required to install drawer slides.

TRADE SECRET

When putting together your hardware order for a set of cabinets, don't forget the slide hardware that will be required for pullout drawers and trays in base cabinets. (See Chapter 12.) The drawer slides used for this application are typically side-mount, over-travel slides that run on ball bearings.

A Different Way to Install Drawer-Slide Hardware

When I'm installing side-mount slides, I often build a plywood U-shaped frame that is sized to hold the slide hardware. (See the photos at right.) Fasten the hardware to the inside of the frame and to the sides of the drawer box, as described below. Then fasten the frame to the sides and back of the case. This can be done easily if you cut and install wood spacer blocks to fill any gaps between the outside of the frame and the sides or back of the box. This installation technique works for side-mount and ball-bearing slides and for bottom-mount nylon roller slides.

A U-shaped wooden frame can be used to install side-mount drawer slides in a face-frame cabinet.

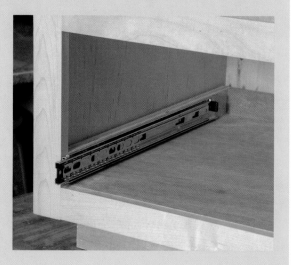

With its hardware attached, the U-shaped frame is installed inside the cabinet.

1. Attach the box part of the slide to the drawer box. Using the screws supplied with the hardware, fasten the box part of the slide to the side or bottom of the drawer box. (See the bottom photo on p. 129.)

2. Install the cabinet half of the slide. This part of the slide mechanism is usually screwed to the face frame and then secured to the back of the cabinet with a rear-mounting socket. In the top photo on p. 128, you can see the slotted installation flanges on this half of the slide mechanism. The slotted flanges allow the slide to flex slightly should the clearance between the hardware and the drawer box be less than perfect. If possible, drive the first installation screws in these slotted flanges. At this stage, it's best to drive only two or three installation screws in each slide.

3. Fine-tune the installation. Fit the drawer half of the hardware into the cabinet-mounted part of the mechanism, then try sliding the drawer box in and out. You'll need to adjust the position of the hardware if the front of the box is skewed or uneven when it closes. When the slide action is smooth and even, drive the remaining installation screws in the round installation holes.

Find the center point of the drawer front by crossing the diagonal lines.

Knobs and Pulls

When it's time to select knobs, handles, and pulls for the doors and drawer fronts in your kitchen, your choices are limited only by the number of catalogs you are willing to look through. You can choose from a tremendous selection of styles, shapes, and materials.

To install knobs and pulls, all you need to do is drill holes for the installation screws. Pulls are more time-consuming because they require two holes. These holes are usually spaced on 3-in. centers. Knobs and pulls for drawers are usually centered on the drawer front. To find the center of a drawer front, mark the point where the diagonals cross. (See the photo above.)

Where you mount knobs and pulls on doors depends on your personal preference. Some people like knobs and pulls to be centered on the door stile; others prefer them on the upper and lower corners of the doors. For the sake of appearance, the placement must be consistent. To find the exact hole placement quickly, use a drilling jig that indexes against a corner of the door. The jig I use is a store-bought version, but you can easily make your own from scrap wood. (See the photo at right.)

A drilling jig makes it easy to drill holes for door pulls in exactly the same spot on each door.

WHAT CAN GO WRONG

A problem can arise when a knob (or pull) is installed in a drawer front and the front is then screwed to the drawer box. This makes the installation screw inaccessible. When the knob loosens over time, the entire drawer front must be removed to retighten the screw. To avoid this inconvenience, I drill an installation hole through both the drawer front and the front of the drawer box. Then I install screws long enough to extend through both layers. A #8 × 32 machine screw will fit all standard knobs and pulls; you can buy whatever length you need.

Clamped to the cabinet, horizontal and vertical guide boards make it easy to align the drawer fronts on their boxes.

Attaching Drawer Fronts

When the drawer-slide hardware has been installed and you've drilled the drawer fronts for their knobs or pulls, it's time to attach the fronts to the boxes. This work can go quickly if you are able to clamp some alignment boards to the cabinet and have a nailer to tack each front to its box.

1. Clamp the alignment boards to the cabinet. As shown in the photo above, these boards keep the fronts vertically and horizontally aligned while you attach them to their boxes. If the drawer fronts are sized to overlay the face frame by ½ in., your alignment boards should be set to that overlay.

2. Tack the drawer box to the drawer front. With the drawer closed, hold the front against the box with one hand, keeping the edges of the front against the guide boards. With your other hand, shoot a couple of short finishing nails through the front of the box and into the front of the drawer. (See the top left photo on the facing page.) This tacking step simply secures the drawer front until you can drive the screws (the next step). If you don't have a nailer, you'll need to do the next step with the drawer closed.

3. Screw the front to the box. Open the drawer partway and drive four screws (one near each corner) through the box front and into the drawer front, as shown in the top right photo on the facing page.

4. Install the knob or pull. At this stage, all drawer fronts should have been drilled for knob or pull installation screws. Continue each hole so that it extends through the front of the drawer box, then install the knob or pull. (See the bottom left photo on the facing page.) Once this is done, you can relocate the horizontal guide board to install the next drawer front.

With a nailer, drive a couple of finishing nails to tack the box to the front.

Install the front by driving a screw through each corner of the box front.

Bore through both fronts to install the knob or pull.

Reposition the horizontal guide board to align the next drawer front.

Accessories

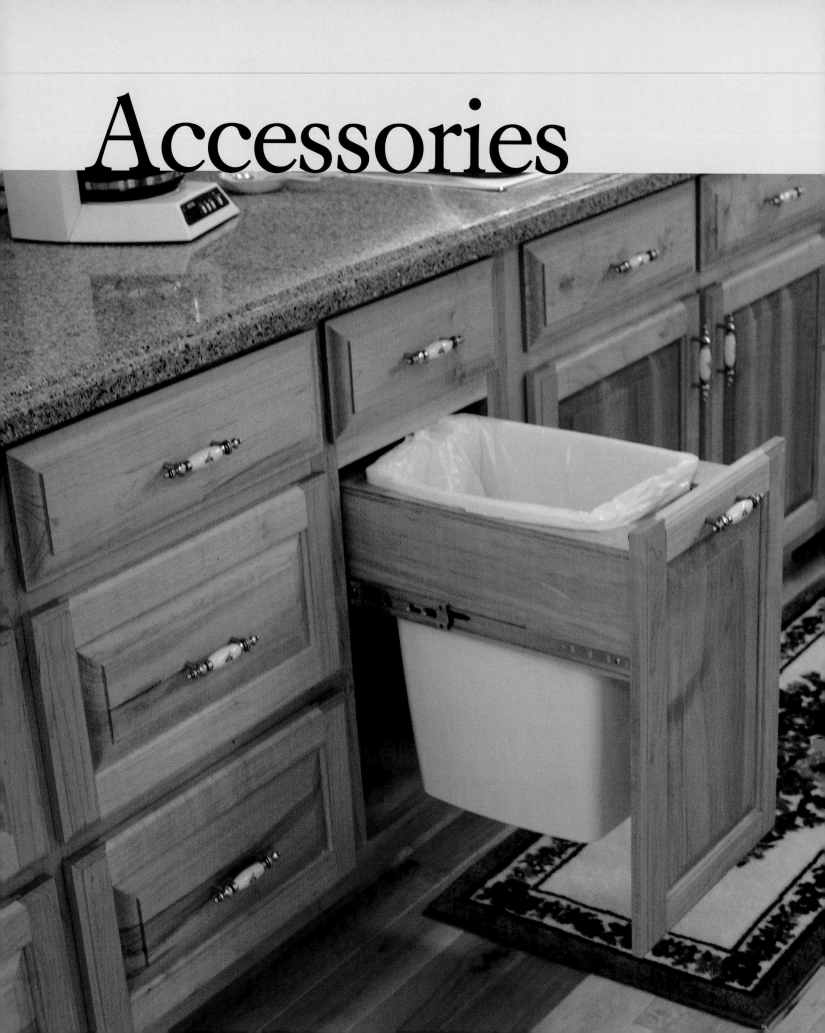

CHAPTER TWELVE

We expect a kitchen of custom-built cabinets to be beautiful. But the new cabinetry must also be easy and convenient to use. This is where accessories come in. Some of these are essential—adjustable shelves, for example. The value of other accessories depends on the preferences of those who will be working in the kitchen.

Many cabinet accessories are associated with specialty hardware that is available through mail-order sources and at woodworking and cabinetry supply outlets. In addition to the hardware covered in this chapter, you'll find a wealth of other organizers and aids that may be useful. As you select each component, make sure the specifications match the size and load-bearing requirements for the planned application. And stick with quality goods that will work reliably and accurately for a long time.

1 Shelves and Shelf Supports, p. 136

2 Sink Trays, p. 140

3 Trash Doors, p. 141

4 Rollout Shelves, p. 142

5 Lazy Susans, p. 142

6 Appliance Garages, p. 143

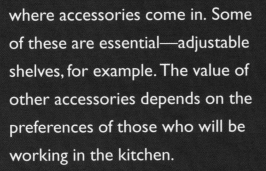

PRO TIP

For shelves longer than 36 in., provide mid-span support by installing shelf supports on the inside of the face frame's center stiles.

TRADE SECRET

To cut slots for installing plastic T-molding on cabinet shelves, you can use an expensive 5/64-in. slot-cutting bit in your router table, or you can pay a lot less for a 7¼-in. circular saw blade that runs in your table saw. DeWalt's thin-kerf, 24-tooth framing blade (a series 20 blade) will do the job, and it costs about $7. Set the height of the blade to about 9/16 in., and adjust the rip fence on your table saw to guide the shelf. Do some test cuts to make sure the slot is centered in the shelf's edge.

Shelves and Shelf Supports

Cabinet shelves are either fixed or adjustable. The only time I use fixed shelves is on cabinets with mullioned glass doors. (See Chapter 8.) Otherwise, it's better for shelves to be adjustable. Shelf material should always be ¾-in. plywood or solid wood. Never use particleboard for shelving; it will sag under its own weight.

Edge treatment options

While a solid wood shelf just needs to be sanded and finished, a plywood shelf requires some sort of edge treatment to cover its plied front edge. There are several options to consider.

Plastic edging. This treatment has become a favorite of mine because plastic T-molding is inexpensive, easy to install, and more durable than wood edgebanding. Different colors of edging are available. To install it, cut a shallow groove down the center of the shelf's front edge. Then tap the molding's barbed flange into the groove. At the ends of the shelf, trim the edging flush with a utility knife. (See the photos below.) Since most of this molding is 13/16 in. wide, it may extend slightly beyond the corners of the plywood. You can trim it flush with a razor or a special edge-trimming tool, available where the molding is sold.

Wood edge banding. This thin wood edging has a heat-activated adhesive applied to one side, so it can simply be ironed onto a plywood edge. Pick an edge banding wood species that's compatible with the face veneer on your shelving. Use an iron and a low heat setting. (See

Install plastic T-molding by tapping the flange into a slot cut in the front edge of the shelf.

Use a utility knife to trim the molding flush with each shelf's edge.

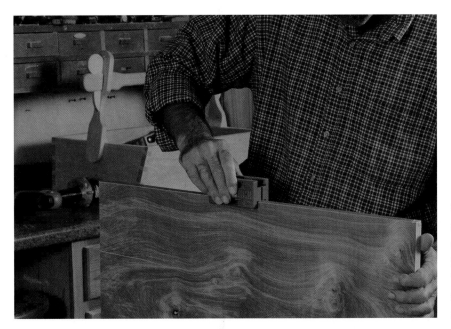

With a double-edge trimmer, trim the long edges of the molding flush with the plywood. This type of trimmer also works well on wood edgebanding.

Solid Wood Edging Options for Plywood Shelves

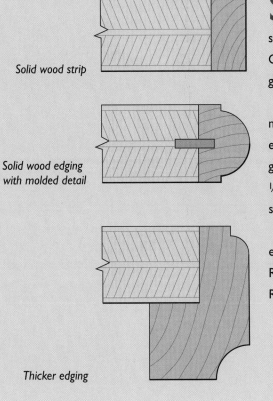

Solid wood strip

Solid wood edging with molded detail

Thicker edging

Solid wood strip edging can be cut on a table saw, then glued to the front edges of plywood shelves. Make this edging 1/4 in. to 3/8 in. thick. Clamp it in place, then sand it smooth after the glue dries.

Molded edging looks elegant and isn't difficult to make. Rout a decorative profile in solid wood edging, either before of after the edging has been glued to the plywood. If the edging is thicker than 1/2 in., it's a good idea to use small biscuits or splines when gluing it to the plywood.

Thicker edging can be used to stiffen a shelf that extends more than 24 in. between supports. Rabbeting the edging makes it easier to install. Routing the front corners improves the appearance.

PRO TIP

For pullout shelves that will hold heavy dishes or pots, consider gluing plastic laminate to the plywood for improved durability.

Wood edgebanding is backed with hot-melt adhesive, so it can be ironed on to the front edge of a plywood shelf.

IN DETAIL

Open shelves can easily be converted into a wine rack by boring holes in some wide boards and then ripping them in half lengthwise. Cut each board to length first; it should span the width of the shelf opening. Bore small holes for bottlenecks and large holes for bottle bases.

IN DETAIL

Instead of buying factory-made drawer dividers, why not make your own? An excellent way to make use of left over wood, these dividers allow you to continue the custom-built theme of your cabinetry.

After trimming off the ends of wood edgebanding, sand the banding edges flush with the plywood.

the top photo above.) Trim the ends flush, then use fine sandpaper (120 or 180 grit) to sand and smooth the front corners, as shown in the bottom photo above.

Solid wood edging. It's more time-consuming to make and install your own edging, but some woodworkers prefer this option. See the sidebar on p. 137 for some shop-made edging ideas.

Shelf supports

There are several types of adjustable shelf supports. The least expensive system uses metal or plastic supports that fit into holes bored in the case sides. The end of each shelf rests on two supports, as shown in the top photo on the facing page. Woodworking suppliers sell supports sized to fit ¼-in.-dia. and 5 mil-dia. holes; the supports are available in both pin and L-bracket styles.

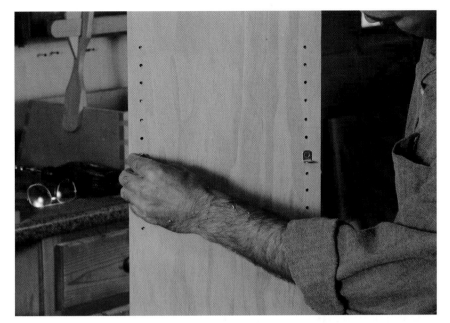

Shelf support clips should fit snugly in their holes.

Drilling holes for shelf clips is easy if you use a template. Always position the template at the bottom end of the side panel to ensure consistent hole spacing.

It's easier to bore shelf support holes before the cabinet cases are assembled. Although factory-made shelf-drilling templates are available, it's not difficult to make your own on a drill press. (See the photo at right.) Make sure you orient the template in the same direction for all four rows of each cabinet.

If you don't want to drill holes in the sides of the cabinets, you can use shelving standards. Four standards are required to support the shelves in a cabinet. My favorite type of standard is a new plastic version that incorporates built-in shelf supports that you can push in or out with the tip of your finger. (See the top photo on p. 140.) These standards can be cut to length with any saw, and they enable you to change a shelf's height almost instantly. Metal standards are also available; they have brass or chrome surface finishes and match-

IN DETAIL

You can mount a pullout garbage can in an inverted drawer that's secured to a door. The drawer bottom faces up with a cutout that's sized to hold a plastic garbage container for the top of the trash can in a trash door (see main text). When making the cutout, include a clearance hole for your hand so that the container will be easy to remove.

Plastic shelving standards have built-in shelf supports, making shelf adjustments easy.

ing support clips that you reposition to change the height of a shelf.

Although standards can be simply tacked to the inside surface of the case side, I prefer to recess each standard in a routed groove. I use an edge guide in my router and set the bit's depth to match the thickness of the standard. (See the photo below.) Make sure you install each set of four standards so that the same ends face up and the shelves will be level.

Sink Trays

These tilt-out trays transform the dead space in front of your sink into a useful storage area for small items like sponges, can openers, and such. (See the top photo on the facing page.) Normally, the upper front area of a sink base cabinet is covered by a pair of drawer fronts. There are no drawer boxes, however, because the sink is in the way. The sink tray kits available at home centers and hardware suppliers include a plastic tray that

To recess metal shelving standards, rout grooves in the sides of the case before you assemble it.

The hinges and the plastic tray are fastened to the drawer front on the sink's base cabinet.

attaches to the inside face of the drawer front and a pair of hinges that are screwed to the face frame. If you have the choice, pick the Euro-style tilt hinges over the traditional scissor hinges. The Euro hinges are a little more expensive, but they are more solid and work more smoothly.

Trash Doors

One accessory I incorporate into all the kitchen cabinets I build is a trash door. Instead of opening a door and then pulling out a waste basket, the basket fits into a drawer box that's mounted on a cabinet door. (See the photo at right.) Although special hardware kits are now available for trash doors, it's not difficult to build your own door using side-mount drawer slides. Make sure you buy over-travel slides so you won't have any trouble removing and replacing the trash can. To hold a standard rectangular garbage can, you'll need a door opening that is 14 in. wide by 20 in. high. I suggest you buy your trash cans ahead of time to make sure the opening will be the right size.

A pullout trash can is very convenient. Make one by building an upside-down drawer box with a cutout for the can, then attach the box to a door.

PRO TIP

If you're planning to build an appliance garage, make sure you have an electrical outlet where the cabinet will be located.

IN DETAIL

A pull-out cutting board is a handy accessory you can build into a base cabinet. Start by gluing up hardwood strips with waterproof glue. Size the cutting board to fit into a drawer opening. Install the drawer slides as you would for any other drawer. The drawer front can be attached with pocket hole screws from the bottom of the cutting board.

To build this accessory, construct a drawer box with sides about 4 in. high. (See Chapter 6.) Make a cutout in the bottom where the garbage can will fit. Using your slide hardware, mount the box upside-down in the opening. The top edges of the box should be about 1 in. down from the top of the opening. Then screw the front of the box to the back of the cabinet door. If you recycle, you may want to designate two or more doors for trash cans.

Rollout Shelves

All my customers ask me to install rollout shelves in their base cabinets. (See the photo below.) Whether these are open shelves, trays with shallow sides, or drawer boxes, the major benefit doesn't change: You don't have to stoop down or kneel on the floor to reach deep into the back of the cabinet. Sometimes I convince a customer

simply to have a base cabinet with deep drawers instead of doors and rollout shelves. Other times, I install doors that conceal these convenient shelves. A pantry cabinet is also a good place for rollout shelves.

You can build and install these shelves just like drawer boxes. Adjust the depth of each shelf so it doesn't interfere with the cabinet's door. To maximize convenience, consider using over-travel slide hardware.

Lazy Susans

Today, homeowners expect both wall and base corner cabinets to be fitted with lazy Susan hardware. These round shelves spin around a center pole that's anchored to the top and bottom of the case. (See the top photo on the facing page.) When you compare the convenience offered by a lazy Susan to the aggravation of groping deep into

Installed with side-mount slide hardware, rollout trays provide easy access to base cabinet storage.

the back of a corner cabinet, it's easy to understand why this accessory is an important one.

Although it's possible to build a lazy Susan, manufactured versions are reasonably priced and fairly easy to install. However, a lazy Susan must be installed while the corner case is being built. For the corner base cabinets described in Chapter 7, use a 24-in. kidney-shaped lazy Susan. For corner wall cabinets (see Chapter 8), use an 18-in. round lazy Susan. Standard kits come with all the hardware but only two shelves. That is sufficient for corner base cabinets. However, if you want more than two shelves, such as for tall corner wall cabinets, you need to buy two kits.

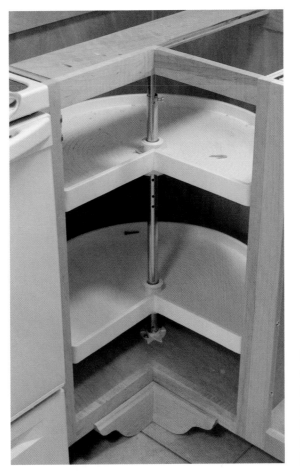

Lazy Susan shelves make corner cabinets much more accessible. The pole and shelves are sold in kit form and must be installed when the case is assembled.

Appliance Garages

As the name suggests, an appliance garage is a separate cabinet designed to keep portable appliances (blenders and food processors, for example) out of sight but ready to use. (See the bottom photo at right.) This optional cabinetry is built to fit between the countertop and the bottom of a wall cabinet. Most of the time, the garage is located in a corner, but it can be placed just about anywhere.

Appliance garage cabinets typically have tambour rolltop doors. Many woodworking and hardware supply stores sell kits that include the tracks as well as the tambour (narrow slats of wood or other material which are glued to a fabric backing). The tambour can be cut on a table saw to fit openings of different widths. If you haven't built one of these units before, my advice is to install the rest of your cabinets, then take your time with the appliance garage. It can be built to fit in the space you select, then installed after your kitchen is otherwise complete.

An appliance garage keeps portable appliances out of sight but accessible. This type of cabinet can be added after the countertop and other cabinets are installed.

Installation

CHAPTER THIRTEEN

You've built your cabinets one by one, and they look great. Now it's time to put the whole project together. Cabinet installation can be a straightforward job or a pain in the neck. It depends on how square the corners are, how plumb and flat the walls are, and how level the floor is. If you don't encounter perfect conditions, don't be too upset; there are well-established ways to compensate so that the finished installation still looks first-rate. You'll also have an easier time if other kitchen remodeling work has already been completed. (See the sidebar on p. 147.)

Even small cabinets are troublesome to move around, so get a helper. With two at work, one person can jockey a cabinet into position while the other drives screws or tightens clamps to keep it there.

1 Plumb, Level, and Square, p. 146

2 Shimming, Scribing, and Trimming, p. 147

3 Installing Wall Cabinets, p. 149

4 Installing Base Cabinets, p. 150

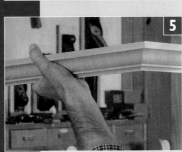

5 Crown Molding and Kickspace Trim, p. 151

TRADE SECRET

Screwed to the wall, a 2×4 makes a great temporary support for installing wall cabinets. Drive screws where their holes won't be seen after the cabinets are installed. The top of the 2×4 should support the bottom of the cabinet at its installed level.

Mark level lines on the wall where the back edges of the cabinets will go.

Plumb, Level, and Square

It's important to check the surfaces against which your cabinets will fit. A 4-ft. level and a framing square are the main tools I use to do this.

- **Test inside corners for square.** Put your framing square into the corner at four or five different elevations and note how far out of square the corner is at each location. If a corner is out of square, it's usually better if it is less than 90 degrees instead of more than 90 degrees.

- **Check walls for plumb.** Do this on each side of the corner, then every 4 ft. or so. While you're checking for plumb, note any high or

Tools and Tips for Finding Studs

To install cabinets or just about anything else against a wood-frame wall, you need to know where the studs are located. The easiest way to find studs is with an electronic stud finder. These handheld devices are affordable and accurate. Most of the time, you should be able to detect the 1½-in. thickness of a stud. Because studs are typically spaced on 16-in. or 24-in. centers, finding one stud tells you where to look for others.

If you don't have a stud finder, there are a few non-electronic detection techniques you can use. A nail or a puttied-over nail hole near the top of baseboard trim often indicates a stud location. The boxes for wall-mounted outlets and switches are nailed to studs, so you'll find one next to a switch or a receptacle. Sometimes it's even possible to see where drywall nails or screws have been driven into studs and then covered with compound—especially when a wall receives light at a sharp angle. To test for a stud location, tap a 6d fin-

An electronic stud finder is a handy tool for marking stud locations.

ishing nail into the wall in a spot that will be covered after the cabinets are installed. It's easy to tell the difference between nailing into a stud and hitting thin air.

low spots on the wall. You can write the specifics of the deviations on parts of the wall that will be covered by cabinets.

- **Test the floor for level.** Working with your 4-ft. level, test floor areas near the wall and about 18 in. out from the wall, where the base of the cabinet will set. Find the highest part of the floor.

- **Mark level layout lines.** If your base cabinets are 35¼ in. high, measure that distance up from the floor's high spot, and make a mark on the wall. Now scribe a level layout line from that mark to show where the back edges of the base cabinets should set. (See the top photo on the facing page.) Mark level layout lines for the wall cabinets as well. You can mark either where the top edges of the wall cabinets will fit or where the bottom edges should align. It's easier to use the lower layout line, but you may not want to leave a pencil mark on the wall.

- **Mark cabinet and stud locations.** When you've marked your level layout lines for the wall and base cabinets, use your tape measure to mark on these lines where each cabinet unit will be located. This will enable you to confirm that the cabinets are positioned properly relative to the planned locations for the stove, refrigerator, dishwasher, and other appliances and fixtures. Also, check to make sure that your rough wiring work is complete.

- **Complete your layout work by marking the stud locations.** I rely on an electronic stud finder, but there are other methods that work equally well. (See the sidebar on the facing page.)

Project Planning: Putting Cabinets in Context

If new cabinets are part of a major kitchen remodeling project, there are a few remodeling tasks you'll want to complete *before* installing your cabinets. If possible, do all the rough wiring work while the walls are bare. Trace a rough outline on kitchen walls to show where the cabinets will be installed, then make sure the rough wiring for receptacles, lights, and appliances is properly located. Pay attention to wall outlet locations—they shouldn't interfere with the countertop backsplash. Make sure you have under-sink receptacles for the garbage disposal and dishwasher. The rough plumbing lines should also be run prior to cabinet installation.

If a new kitchen floor is part of the project, it's better to install the new flooring before installing the cabinets. The new floor will go down faster and won't reduce the height of the countertop.

Shimming, Scribing, and Trimming

Before you begin installing cabinets, it's good to have some idea of how you plan to compensate for surfaces that are less than plumb, level, and square. If a wall is ½ in. or more out of square over the length of the installation, I follow the wall surface when installing cabinets to avoid a major gap at the end of the run. This means that the stiles of some adjoining face frames will have to be

If the gap between the back of the cabinet and the wall is too big to be filled with caulk, cover the gap with a small piece of molding.

PRO TIP

When installing a shim between the back of a cabinet and the wall, try to place it near a stud.

IN DETAIL

Back-beveling is a technique designed to create a tight fit on the front, or "show" side, of a joint. As shown in the drawing below, the joining edges are planed back slightly so that contact is made along the front of the joint. This allows both parts to be clamped together tightly or—if necessary—trimmed for a tighter fit.

Back side: The joint is back-beveled

"Show" side: The joint is tight

TRADE SECRET

Precut wood shims are available at most lumberyards and building-supply outlets. The trouble with these shims is that they are tapered. While it's fast and easy to slide a tapered shim into place, such a shim only provides support along a narrow line. For more solid support, cut your own shims to fit. This takes a little longer but results in a more solid support. A dab of glue ensures that the shim will stay in place.

beveled slightly to eliminate gaps. (See In Detail at left.)

It's almost certain that the face-frame joints on the corner cabinet will need some "tuning" in order to fit tightly. I make these adjustments using a sharp, low-angle block plane. With the blade set to take a very light shaving, you can plane just the right amount from the adjoining stiles. Here's where you'll appreciate having used straight-grained wood for face frames: It planes smoothly.

Your second option is to join cabinets together straight and square. I do this when the wall is less than ½ in. out of square. If there is a slight gap between the back of the end cabinet and the wall, it can be covered with a small molding. I really believe that moldings were invented not for decorative proposes but to hide imperfections. (See the photo on p. 147.)

When you join cabinets so they are straight and square, you'll probably need to install shims in

Wall Cabinet Installation

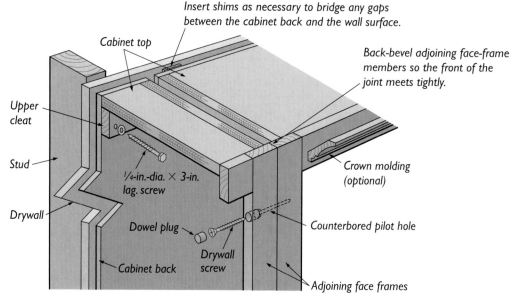

Insert shims as necessary to bridge any gaps between the cabinet back and the wall surface.

Cabinet top

Back-bevel adjoining face-frame members so the front of the joint meets tightly.

Upper cleat

Stud

¼-in.-dia. × 3-in. lag. screw

Drywall

Dowel plug

Drywall screw

Cabinet back

Crown molding (optional)

Counterbored pilot hole

Adjoining face frames

Base Cabinet Installation

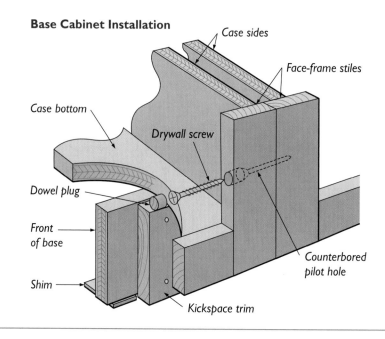

Case sides

Face-frame stiles

Case bottom

Drywall screw

Dowel plug

Front of base

Shim

Counterbored pilot hole

Kickspace trim

areas where the wall and floor surfaces do not meet the cabinet edges. It's not necessary to completely fill a gap with shim material. But the shim should fit snugly in place and support the cabinet so it remains plumb and level, without wobbling. As shown in the drawings on the facing page, the shims are used between the cabinet and the wall and (with base cabinets) between the cabinet base and the floor. When your installation job is finished, the shims should either be out of sight or hidden by covering material.

Installing Wall Cabinets

I like to install wall cabinets first, and I usually begin with the corner cabinet. (See the photo at right.) With assistance from one or two helpers, lift the corner cabinet against its layout lines on the wall. Hold it in place by driving a couple of 3-in. drywall screws through the top cleats and into the studs. Now check the cabinet for level and plumb by placing your level across the top of the cabinet and against both face-frame stiles. As necessary, insert shims between the back of the cabinet and the wall to get the installation plumb and level. Drive installation screws through the bottom cleats and recheck for plumb and level.

Now you can install the adjoining wall cabinets. If you need to make cutouts in a cabinet for a wall outlet or vent, do so before installing the cabinet. The face frames of adjoining cabinets should go together without any noticeable gaps, whether they fit solidly against the wall or require shimming, as described above. It may be necessary to back-bevel the edge of a stile so that the joint between the stiles fits tightly. (See In Detail on the facing page.)

Drive a couple of installation screws through the cabinet's top cleat to hold it in position. Clamp together adjoining face-frame members

Install corner cabinets first. Check for plumb by placing a level against a face-frame stile.

and check the cabinet for plumb and level. Install shims as necessary and drive installation screws in the cabinet's bottom cleat. With clamps still on the adjoining face frames, drill counterbored pilot holes and screw the joint fast with 2-in. or 2½-in. drywall screws.

Working your way out from the corner, continue installing wall cabinets until you're done. If your measurements and layout are correct, the wall cabinets should tie into a tall pantry cabinet at the same height. If everything looks fine, you can make the installation permanent by replacing the drywall screws in the top cleat with ¼-in.-dia. by 3½-in. lag screws. The extra holding power of the lag screws will give you confidence that the cabinets will stay put no matter how they are loaded. There's no need to use lag screws in the bottom cleats.

Give the face frame a final check to make sure the joints are sound, then fill each counterbored hole with a wood plug that is glued in place. Cut and sand the plugs flush after the glue dries.

PRO TIP

Wood or plastic pads, placed beneath clamp feet, protect the face-frame surfaces when adjacent cabinets are clamped together.

WHAT CAN GO WRONG

When a base cabinet needs to be shimmed out from the wall, installing countertops with built-up edges can be difficult. Before you install base cabinets, know how much shim space is available behind the cabinet before the countertop's built-up front edge interferes with the front of the cabinet.

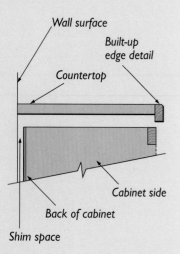

Wall surface

Built-up
edge detail

Countertop

Cabinet side

Back of cabinet

Shim space

Install spacer blocks to tie a corner base cabinet to the wall framing. Cut each block to fit after getting the cabinet plumb and level.

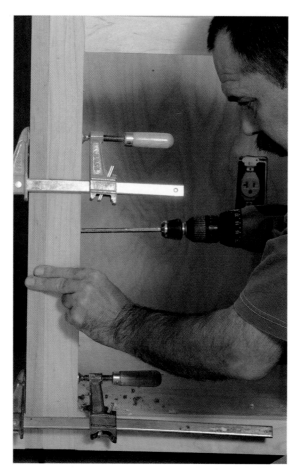

Clamp together cabinet face frames, then secure the joint with counterbored screws.

Installing Base Cabinets

Like wall cabinet installation, base cabinet installation also starts in the corners. Position the corner case so that the front of the face frame is 24 in. away from both walls. The back of the case will be 5½ in. to 6 in. from the wall. To tie the case to the wall, you'll need to install ¾-in. plywood spacer blocks, as shown in the photo above. But before cutting these blocks to size, make sure you get the case level and plumb by inserting shims, as necessary, beneath the base. Screw the spacer blocks to the back of the case and to one or more studs.

Once the corner base cabinet has been done, install the adjacent unit and work your way out from the corner, just as you did with the wall cabinets. Clamp together adjoining face frames before driving counterbored screws to hold them fast. (See the photo at left.) Install shims, as necessary, between the cabinet back and the wall, and between the floor and the base, to get each cabinet plumb and level. Then anchor the cabinet in place by driving 3-in. drywall screws through the upper cleat and into a stud. (See the top photo on the facing page.) Some base cabinets will require

To install a standard base cabinet, drive a 3-in. drywall screw through the cleat and into a stud.

cutouts for electrical outlets and plumbing. (See the photo at right.) I don't know of a foolproof system for making these cutouts, so I fall back on some proven advice: Measure twice and cut once.

When all the cabinets have been firmly secured to the walls and to each other, do any fine-tuning work that's required. All dowel plugs glued in counterbored holes need to be trimmed flush, sanded, and spot-finished. Face frames that are not quite flush should also be sanded and finished. Fill small holes with wood putty. If you have a long gap that still remains despite your fine-tuning work, cover it with a small piece of molding made from wood of the same species.

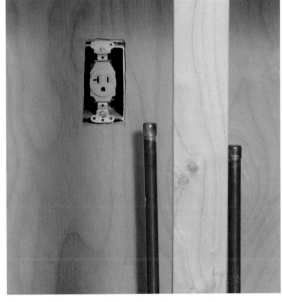

Determining cutout locations for electrical and plumbing lines can be a challenge.

Crown Molding and Kickspace Trim

There are several ways to trim out the kickspace. (See the sidebar on p. 153.) All treatments are designed to cover the front base pieces of adjoining base cabinets. I like to cut kickspace trim from the same species of wood used for the face frames. Use long boards, if possible, for a seamless appearance. Prefinish all kickspace trim before installing it with 6d finishing nails.

Not all wall cabinets need to be finished off with a crown molding. But I think that this finishing touch improves the appearance of your cabinets by tying the installation together and giving it the look of a fine piece of furniture. Whether you use a stock crown molding or make your own, many variations are possible. It's even possible to combine stock and shop-made molding treatments. (See In Detail on p. 152.)

IN DETAIL

There's plenty of room for creativity when designing a crown molding treatment to finish off the top of wall cabinets. The drawing below shows one of many ways that a combination of moldings can be used.

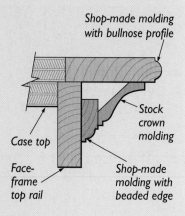

Shop-made molding with bullnose profile

Stock crown molding

Case top

Face-frame top rail

Shop-made molding with beaded edge

TRADE SECRET

If you're planning to finish off wall cabinets with crown molding, always start with about 25% more material than the linear foot measure demands. You'll need the extra if any miters have to be recut. Save the longest pieces of molding to extend across the front of a wall of cabinets so you can avoid unsightly butt joints.

To install crown molding, you need a chopsaw equipped with a finish-cutting blade. My technique is to forget all that complicated stuff about compound angles and positioning moldings upside-down on the saw. Instead, I attach an auxiliary fence to the saw to hold the molding in its installed position. (See the photo below.) The miter cuts you make in the auxiliary fence enable you to align the blade with the marks you make on your crown molding.

Installing crown molding takes concentration and patience. Depending on how a cabinet fits in the overall installation, it's sometimes smart to install some or all of the crown molding before installing the cabinet. Whether I'm working on a single cabinet or a series of installed cabinets, I usually start in one corner and work my way

around. Don't use your tape measure to mark cut lines. Instead, hold the molding in its installed position, and use a sharp pencil to mark exactly where the straight or miter cut must be. For ease in handling, you may want to cut a piece of molding to rough length before marking and cutting.

Test-fit each joint as you go. (See the photo on the facing page.) If you encounter a corner that isn't square, you may need to nudge the saw's cutting angle slightly one way or the other to get the fit right. Don't be surprised if you have to discard a miscut piece and start over—that's why smart woodworkers always have more molding than they need. After the final cutting, tack each piece in place with just a couple of brads or small finishing nails; don't drive them all the way in at this point.

With an angled auxiliary fence attached to a chopsaw, the crown molding is held in its installed position while the miter cuts are made.

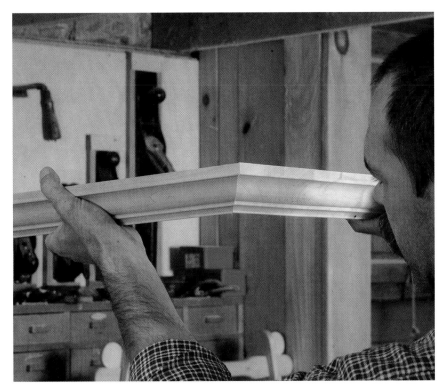

Test-fit a crown molding miter joint before you install the molding.

When the last piece has been tacked in place and you're happy with the fit, go back and do the final installation. I usually use a light coat of glue on miter joints, except for where the molding joins the cabinet. Make sure you set all finishing nails used to install the molding and fill the holes with putty.

With the heavy lifting and exacting joinery work done, the last thing to do is install the doors and drawers. If you use Euro-style cup hinges for doors and ball-bearing slides for drawers (as I do), you'll have an easier time installing the doors and drawers. See Chapter 11 for details.

Kickspace Options

I like to finish off the kickspace with a solid board of the same wood species used in the cabinet's face frame. This ¾-in.-thick board is cut to fit the kickspace opening. It covers the gaps between adjacent cabinets as well as any gaps created by shims used to level the cabinet. Some people also like to install a quarter-round shoe molding where the kickspace trim meets the floor. Still others prefer to glue a vinyl cove base molding against the kickspace trim. Vinyl trim is used most often with a vinyl floor.

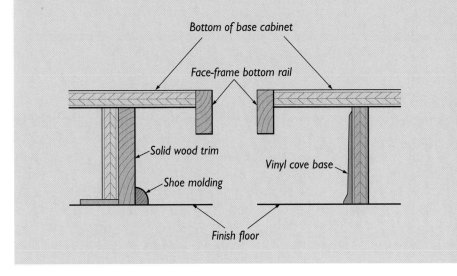

Countertops

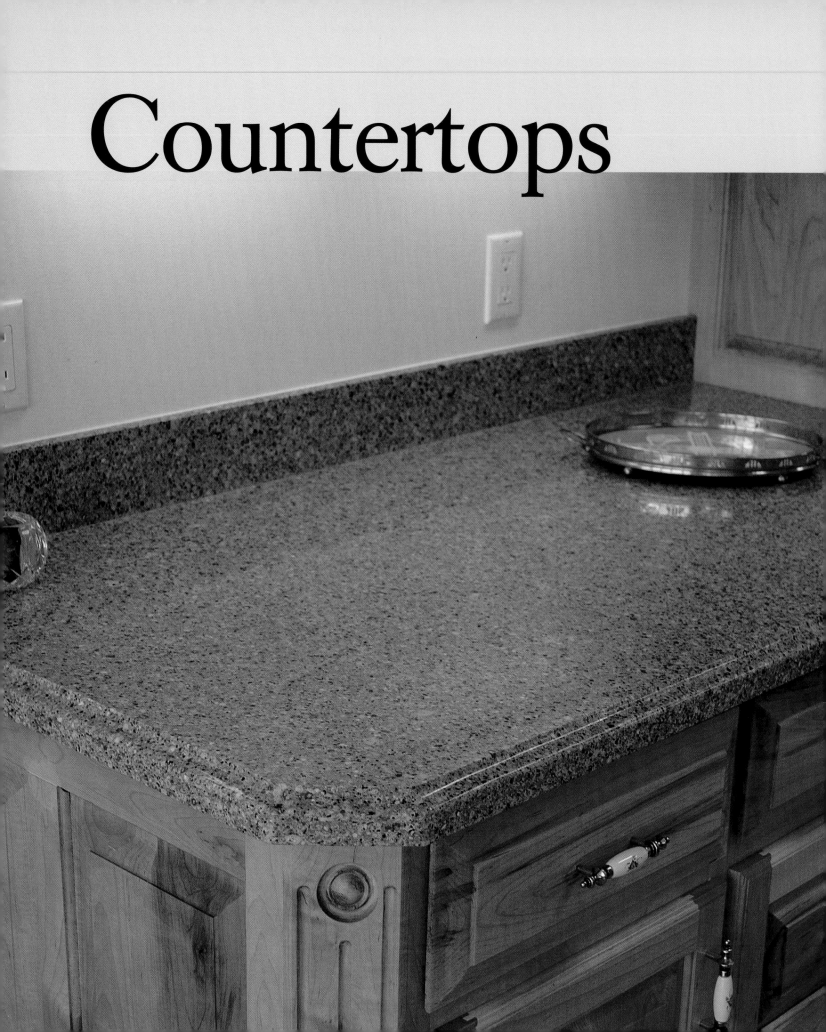

It's not easy to choose a kitchen countertop. There are many types available, and even within each type you have to make decisions about color, texture, style, and design. Although countertop installation is the final step in building new kitchen cabinets, it's good to begin thinking about this finishing touch early in the design process. The countertops you choose need to complement the appearance and style of your cabinets.

Durability and ease of maintenance should figure into your countertop decision. And cost is certain to be important, too. Finally, you'll need to decide how much of the job you want to do yourself. As you'll see in the descriptions that follow, some countertops can be built and installed by a cabinetmaker, while others require professional fabrication and (in some cases) installation.

1 Plastic Laminate, p. 156

2 Solid Surface Material and Engineered Stone, p. 156

3 Granite and Soapstone, p. 160

4 Tile, p. 161

5 Solid Wood, p. 162

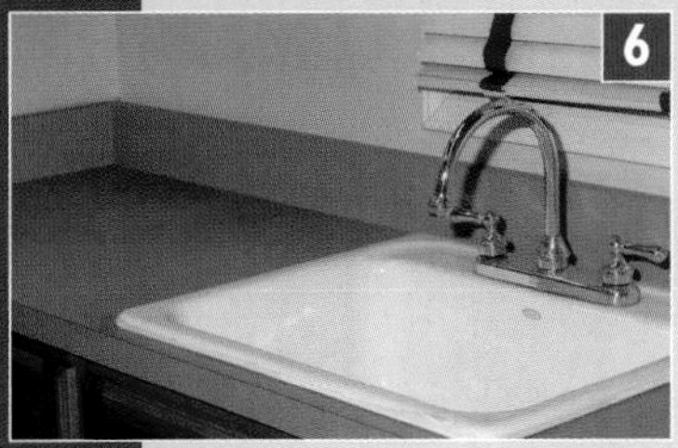

6 Installing Countertops, p. 162

IN DETAIL

Available in a variety of colors and patterns, plastic laminate is made from layers of paper and plastic resin pressed into thin sheets. The color and pattern in the topmost layer of paper are what you see in a finished sheet of laminate. A clear layer of resin forms a protective barrier over the top sheet of paper.

Even though laminate is typically 18% plastic resin and 82% paper, the material has more strength for its weight than steel does. Laminate designed for countertops and other work surfaces is $^1/_{16}$ in. thick. Laminate used on vertical surfaces (cabinet doors, for example) is just $^1/_{32}$ in. thick.

TRADE SECRET

A countertop that is dark in color or finished with a high gloss can be stunning at first glance. But such countertops almost always drive homeowners crazy because of how easily they show scratches, dust, and dirt. The best hues to hide dirt and scratches are natural earth tones. A matte or textured surface finish hides dirt and scratches much better than a glossy surface does.

Solid surface material looks like polished stone but is made from plastic resin and mineral particles. (Photo courtesy Lowe's Home Improvement Store, Franklin, NC.)

Plastic Laminate

This countertop material has been popular for more than 50 years. Even with all the options available, laminate countertops still go into about one-third of all new kitchens. It's easy to appreciate laminate's appeal. No other countertop material offers such a broad selection of colors, textures, and patterns. Whether you want ruby red, stark white, or the appearance of wood or stone, you can be sure it's available.

Plastic laminate is durable and easy to clean. It's also affordable and easy to work with. Anyone with basic woodworking tools can make plastic laminate countertops. Make sure you follow the manufacturer's safety instructions for working with solvent-based contact cement. For a step-by-step construction sequence, see the sidebar on pp. 158-159.

On the down side, the seams between laminate countertop sections are always visible and vulnerable to moisture. Liquid that penetrates between the seams can cause the underlayment to swell. Plastic laminate is not as heat resistant as many other countertop materials. And unlike solid surface material (see below), plastic laminate can't be repaired if it chips, cracks, or becomes scratched.

Solid Surface Material and Engineered Stone

Since its development more than 30 years ago, Corian® solid surface material by DuPont® has established a new standard for custom countertops. (See the photo above.) Today, solid surface choices include Wilsonart Gibraltar®, Formica Fountainhead®, and Avonite®. These materials are manufactured from acrylic or polyester resins and different mineral fillers.

As the name suggests, solid surface material has no separate core or substrate. Because it is nonporous, it is very stain resistant. Corian and similar products have higher heat resistance than laminate, though trivets are always recommended beneath hot pots and pans. Homeowners also like solid surface countertops because there are so many edge treatments available, allowing each countertop to have a distinctive appearance. (See the photo at right.)

Solid surface material typically looks like stone but cuts like wood—exceptionally hard wood. Unless you are trained and certified to fabricate this type of countertop, you'll need to order it from a supplier. You provide the dimensions and select the color or simulated stone effect you want. The supplier will also help you select an edge detail. Upgrade options include backsplash choices and an integral solid surface sink. Expect to pay a premium price. A cost of $100 per running foot is not uncommon. To maintain the manufacturer's warranty, certified fabricators usually install solid surface countertops.

As with solid surface material, engineered stone looks like stone but is man-made; quartz is the primary ingredient. (See the photo below.) Brand names include Silestone®, which is made in Spain and marketed in the U.S. through Cosentino USA. (See Resources on p. 165.) Other manufac-

A number of edge treatments are possible when you order a solid surface countertop. (Photo courtesy Lowe's Home Improvement Store, Franklin, NC.)

A man-made mixture of resin and quartz, engineered stone is even harder than solid surface material.

MAKING A PLASTIC LAMINATE COUNTERTOP

It's not difficult to fabricate a laminate countertop, provided you have a large enough work area. It's important for the countertop's base or substrate to be flat when the laminate is glued to it. Cut the laminate sheet about ½ in. larger than the outside dimensions of the base, and make sure the adhesive-coated surfaces don't come into contact until the laminate is properly positioned over the base.

To build the base for a laminate countertop, fasten a solid wood outside edge to a plywood or particleboard substrate with glue and pocket screws.

Use a random-orbit sander to sand the solid wood edging flush with the top surface of the plywood.

Coat both mating surfaces with contact adhesive, then allow the adhesive to dry.

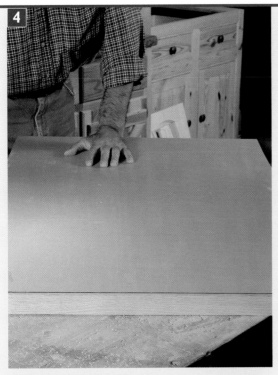

Use dowels or thin sticks to keep the slightly over-size sheet of laminate aligned over the substrate. Remove the spacers one by one and press the laminate onto the plywood.

Working from the center outward, make sure that no air pockets are left under the laminate. Use a block of wood to spread the hammer blow and protect the laminate surface.

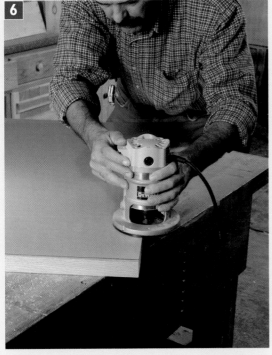

Use a flush-trim bit in a router to trim the edge of the laminate flush with the solid wood edging.

Use a 45-degree chamfer bit to create a nice finished edge.

PRO TIP

When making a tile countertop, buy and store extra tiles in case damaged ones need to be replaced in the future.

IN DETAIL

Tile countertops should be made with nonporous vitreous tile. Porous (nonvitreous) tile absorbs food spills and other moisture, creating conditions where mold can grow. Use latex or acrylic-modified adhesive and grout when installing a tile countertop.

Tile used for the backsplash serves a more decorative purpose and isn't subjected to the same conditions as countertop tile. For a backsplash, it's acceptable to use different types of tile, but keep in mind that vitreous tile will be easier to clean and more stain resistant than other types.

WHAT CAN GO WRONG

Building your countertops before installing your cabinets can lead to a poor fit among these components. To avoid problems, build and install your cabinets before you make or order your countertops. Measure carefully, making sure that built-up countertop edges will clear cabinet fronts and that shim spaces between the base cabinets and the wall will be covered when the countertop and backsplash are installed.

A granite countertop can't be damaged by hot items, but it must be treated with a sealer to ensure stain resistance. (Photo courtesy Lowe's Home Improvement Store, Franklin, NC.)

tures are DuPont, which sells their product as Zodiaq®, and CeasarStone.

Thanks to the hardness of quartz, engineered stone is tougher than solid surface material. It also has excellent stain and chip resistance. Different stone color tones are available, along with a variety of edge treatments. Custom fabrication is the rule for these countertops, and the countertop supplier typically does the installation.

Granite and Soapstone

In recent years, granite has become a popular countertop material in high-end kitchens. (See the photo above.) This naturally occurring rock is composed of feldspar, quartz, and mica and is almost as hard as diamond. It can be polished and sealed to show a high gloss, but matte and other finishes are also possible. The most common edge treatment is a broad roundover, or "bullnose." Hot

pans won't damage a granite countertop, but the surface can become stained, because the material is porous. Stain resistance is maintained by treating the countertop surface with sealer.

You can buy granite countertops from a local supplier or find fabricators online. Prices for standard-size slabs are reasonable (under $30 per sq. ft. from some suppliers), but the labor involved in making sink cutouts and corner joints will increase the installation cost significantly. Granite is most affordable when you have a straight run of base cabinets with no cutouts.

Soapstone has been used as a countertop material for hundreds of years. Composed primarily of talc, soapstone is relatively soft and porous, but it is highly resistant to chemicals and heat. This explains why it has long been used as a countertop in laboratories. At one time, soapstone was heavily mined in Vermont and Virginia. Today, most of it comes from Brazil. The price for this countertop option is around $50.00 per sq. ft.

Tile is the only countertop material that can be installed right in the kitchen. Beneath the tile, plywood and cement board provide a solid substrate.

Tile

Tile countertops never seem to go out of fashion. If you shop around for a good deal, this option can be nearly as inexpensive as plastic laminate. And the creative possibilities are endless when you consider all the tile shapes, styles, and colors available.

Installing a tile countertop involves quite a bit of labor. You have to prepare the substrate, which typically consists of cement backer board screwed over ¾-in. plywood. Some people like

the look of a tile countertop with a solid wood edge treatment; others prefer a tiled edge. A tile countertop has excellent heat and stain resistance, just like more expensive countertops, but the grout is its weak area. It's more prone to staining and cracking than the tile itself, and grout that has become cracked or dislodged must be repaired to prevent moisture from getting under the countertop. Epoxy grout formulations are usually recommended for improved durability.

IN DETAIL

Recent studies have shown that natural wood cutting boards are safer than plastic versions. Even on a heavily scarred board, bacteria does not multiply and eventually dies. Heavily scarred plastic boards are more difficult to clean and enable bacteria to multiply.

Making a cutting board is a great way to use up hardwood scraps. Cut the boards to a pleasing shape, affix them with epoxy or another waterproof glue, and sand the finished product thoroughly to smooth the surfaces and round the corners. Clean the board after use with hot water and dishwashing detergent. To remove odors, squeeze on some lemon juice.

You can make your own butcher-block countertop by gluing up sections as wide as your planer can surface, then gluing those sections together.

Solid Wood

Laminated wood "butcher-block" countertops are beautiful to look at but challenging to maintain. When a wood countertop is used in a kitchen, it's often used selectively for just one section or part of a countertop.

You can buy factory-made wood countertops, but you'll save plenty of money by making your own. Traditional butcher blocks are made from hard rock maple, but you can use other dense, strong woods, including oak and cherry. Depending on its intended use, the surface is treated with a durable finish, such as varnish or polyurethane, or left unfinished for food preparation.

To make a long-lasting, warp-resistant top, use waterproof adhesive to glue up wood strips that are ¾ in. to 1½ in. thick and 2 in. to 2½ in. wide. Thinner strips provide more stability. Build up sections as wide as your thickness planer can accommodate, plane the sections, then glue them together. (See the photo above.) If you plan to varnish the wood, finish-sand the countertop to 220 grit. An unfinished surface will be subject to heavy cleaning and scrubbing, so sanding with 120-grit sandpaper should be fine.

Installing Countertops

This step should go smoothly, as long as your base cabinets are plumb, level, and solidly secured. If the wall surface is irregular or less than straight at countertop height, it may cause a poor fit between the back edge of the countertop and the wall. If you know the wall surface is irregular, choose a countertop that has an applied backsplash. (See the top photo on the facing page.) The backsplash will cover any gaps between the back edge of the countertop and the wall.

The weight of a countertop helps keep it in place, but use fasteners and adhesives to prevent it from shifting. Secure a plastic laminate, tile, or wood countertop by driving screws through the top bracing or cleats in the base cabinets and into the underside of the countertop or countertop substrate. Other countertops are usually secured with a sealant or an adhesive caulk that matches the countertop material.

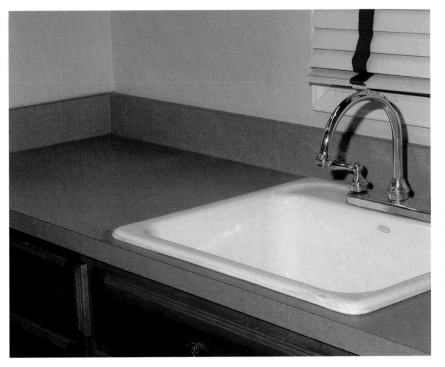

If your walls are irregular or out of square, install a flat laminate top and hide the gaps at the wall with a separate backsplash. (Photo courtesy Lowe's Home Improvement Store, Franklin, NC.)

Other Countertop Options

With a little research, you'll discover other countertop treatments that may be right for a future kitchen project. Concrete countertops are gaining in popularity, especially on the West Coast. These heavyweight countertops can be fabricated off-site or formed and poured in the kitchen after the cabinets have been installed. (See Resources on p. 165.) Stainless steel countertops have long been used in commercial kitchens, and some homeowners choose this indestructible material for their own kitchens. Custom-made by a steel fabricator, stainless steel countertops can include an integral sink and backsplash, along with a rolled front edge.

Whatever countertop choice you make, keep in mind that it doesn't have to be permanent. A good set of kitchen cabinets can outlive a number of different countertops.

A concrete countertop can be built on top of installed cabinets or fabricated offsite.

Resources

CAD (Computer-Aided Design)Software for Kitchens

20-20 Technologies
www.2020design.com

Brøderbund
www.Broderbund.com

Cabinet Vision
www.cabinetvision.com

Chief Architect
www.chiefarch.com

DecoTech 3D Design Software
www.aaWorldSales.com

Kitchen Consultants
www.kitchen-consultants.com

Pragma Informatique
www.KitchenDraw.com

Woodworking Tools, Accessories and Associated Supplies

Eagle America
Outlet Store: 510 Center St.
Chardon, OH 44024
1-800-872-2511
www.eagle-america.com

Grizzly Industrial, Inc.
P.O. Box 2069
Bellingham, WA 98226
1-800-523-4777
www.grizzly.com

Lee Valley Tools
P.O. Box 1780
Ogdensburg, NY 13669-6780
1-800-513-7885
(from Canada & other countries)
1-800-668-1807
P.O. Box 6295, Station J
Ottawa, ON K2A 1T4
www.leevalley.com
Also: hardware, finishing supplies

MLCS (router bits and
shaper cutters)
1-800-533-9298
Showroom & store:
2381 Philmont Ave.
Huntingdon Valley, PA 19006
www.mlcswoodworking.com

Rockler Woodworking
and Hardware
4365 Willow Drive
Medina, MN 55340
1-800-279-4441
www.rockler.com
*Also: hardware, lumber, finishing
supplies*

TOOLS PLUS
153 Meadow St.
Waterbury, CT 06702
1-800-222-6133
www.tools-plus.com/

Woodworker's Supply
5604 Alameda Pl., NE
Albuquerque, NM 87113
1-800-645-9292
www.woodworker.com
Also: hardware, finishing supplies

Woodworkers Warehouse Inc.
Amesbury Industrial Park
10 Industrial Way
Amesbury, MA 01913
Catalog Requests: 800-789-3773
www.thewoodworkingcatalog.com

Woodcraft Supply
Woodcraft
P.O. Box 1686
Parkersburg, WV 26102-1686
1-800-225-1153
*Also: hardware, lumber,
finishing supplies*

Hardware Suppliers

Custom Service Hardware
1170 Wauwatosa Rd.
Cedarburg, WI 53012
Toll-Free: (800)882-0009
http://www.cshardware.com/

Outwater Plastics Industries
East Coast Sales/Warehouse
4 Passaic St.
P.O. Box 403
Wood-Ridge, NJ 07075
1-800-631-8375
www.outwater.com

Van Dyke's
Restorers Division
P.O. Box 278
Woonsocket, SD 57385
Phone: (605) 796-4425
Toll-Free: (800)787-3355

Woodworker's Hardware &
Supply Inc.
5623 E. Washington Blvd.
Los Angeles, CA 90040-1405
Phone: (323) 722-0062

Hardware Manufacturers

Amerock Corp.
4000 Auburn St.
Rockford, IL 61125
1-815-969-6308

Grass America Inc.
1202 Hwy. 66 S.
P.O. Box 1019
Kernersville, NC 27284
1-800-334-3512
www.grassusa.com

Hafele America Co.
3901 Cheyenne Dr.
P.O. Box 4000
Archdale, NC 27263
1-800-423-3531
www.hafeleonline.com

Hettich America L.P.
6225 Shiloh Rd.
Alpharetta, GA 30005
1-800-627-5152

Julius Blum Inc.
Cabinet & Furniture
Hardware Mfg.
7733 Old Plank Rd.
Stanley, NC 28164
1-704-827-1345

Mepla-Alfit Inc.
130 Lexington Parkway
Lexington, NC 27295-8524
1-800-858-4957

Salice America Inc.
2123 Crown Centre Dr.
Charlotte, NC 28227
1-800-222-9652

Index

A

Accessories, 134–143. *See also* Lazy Susans
  appliance garages, 143
  cutting board, pull-out, 142
  rollout shelves, 124, 130, 142
  shelves and shelf supports, 136–140
  sink trays, 140–141
  trash doors, 39–40, 140–142
Air cleaner, 116
Air compressor, 16–17
Angles, measurement of, 98, 104
Appliance garages, 143
Appliances, 147
  base cabinets, sized to fit, 34
  cooktop, 111
  design for, 33–34
  dishwasher, 38
  microwave oven, 108
  refrigerator cabinet, 108–109
  wall ovens, cabinets for, 109–110
Architect's scale, 34
Ash, 120
Assembly table, making, 88

B

Back-beveling, 148
Backsplash, 162–163
Baking sheets, storage of, 41
Bandsaw, 11, 67
Base cabinets, 84–95
  assembling standard cabinets, 87–91
  base frame, 88
  corner cabinets, 91–94, 126
  cutlist, 86–87, 90
  cutting board, pull-out, 142
  cutting panels to size, 87
  end panel cabinets, 94–95
  face frames (*See* Face-frame construction)
  installation, 150–151
  island, 110–111
  partitions for tray storage, 41
  rollout shelves/trays, 124, 130, 142
  trash can, pull-out, 39–40, 140–142
Beaded face frames, 51–53
Bevel gauge, 17
Bevels
  back-beveling, 148
  cabinet installation, beveling stiles for, 147–148
  two bevels, cutting panel with, 73
Biscuit joiner, 15, 90
Biscuit joints, 90–91
  face frames, 51
  wall cabinets, 99–102
Bits, 13, 56. *See also* Router bits
  dovetail, 81
  Vix, 127
Blades, saw. *See* Saw blades
Block plane, 148
Board feet (bd. ft.)
  average kitchen, used in, 26
  calculating, 22
Brad nailer, 16–17, 85
Brushing lacquer, 117–118

C

Cabinets. *See also* Base cabinets; Doors, cabinet;
  Drawers, cabinet; End panel cabinets; Face-
  frame construction; Pantry cabinets; Wall
  cabinets
  assembly table for, 88
  custom, 39–41
  dimensions, 34–36, 40, 43–47, 98, 108, 110
  frameless, 37
  island, 110–111
  labeling parts, 98
  location, determining, 34–36
  project records, 70
  under-cabinet light fixtures, 100
Cabinet saw, 87
Calculator, carpenter's, 56
Case hardening, 27
Cherry, 25–26, 121
Chopsaws, 12–13, 46, 47, 152
Circular saw, 89
Clamping blocks, 102
Clamps
  types of, 17, 48
  use of, 48, 64, 78, 103, 104
Cleats, 101–102
Common grade, 27
Composite-wood panels, 19–24. *See also*
  Plywood
Computer-aided design (CAD), 32–33, 165
Concealed hinges, 124–127, 141
Concrete countertop, 163
Conversion varnish, 116
Cooktop, 111
Cope and stick profiles, 58, 59, 65
Corian®, 156
Corner, 45-degree, 72–73, 94–95
Corner cabinets, 34–35. *See also* Lazy Susans
  angled face frames for, 49–50, 148
  base cabinets, 91–94, 126, 150
  installation, 148–150
  wall cabinets, 97, 104–105, 149
Cost
  cabinet, 34
  countertop, 156, 157, 160, 161
  hardware, 123, 128
  hardwood, 25–26
  plywood, 21
  total kitchen, 33–34
Counter space frontage, determining amount
  of, 32
Countertops, 154–163
  concrete, 163
  granite and soapstone, 160
  installing, 162–163
  plastic laminate, 156, 158–159, 162–163
  solid surface material and engineered
    stone, 156–160
  solid wood, 162
  stainless steel, 163
  tile, 160–162
Crook (lumber defect), 29
Crooked board, straightening, 8
Crown molding, 36, 44, 151–153
Cup (lumber defect), 29
Curved door panels, 41, 55, 56, 65, 67–69
Cutlist, 61
  base cabinets, 86–87, 90
  drawers, 78
  software, 90
  wall cabinets, 98
Cutting board
  making, 162
  pull-out, 142
  wood *vs.* plastic, 162

D

Dehumidifier, 12, 26
Design, 30–41
  appliances, 33–34, 38
  computer-aided, 32–33, 165
  custom cabinets, 39–41
  doors and drawers, 37–39
  drawings, 32–36
  face frame assembly, 45
  ideas, 32, 36
  work triangle, 33

Dishwasher, location of, 38
Display shelves, 41. *See also* Glass-paneled doors
Display space, above cabinets, 36
Doors, cabinet, 37–39, 54–71
  assembling, 67–71
  calculating and cutting parts, 56, 58–61
  curved top (*See* Curved door panels)
  cutlist, 61
  design options, 56–58
  finishing, 72
  glass-paneled, 41, 57, 62–63, 100
  hardware (*See* Hardware)
  inset, 52, 125
  joinery details, 57
  milling of door parts, 61–67
  project records, 70
  Spaceballs™, use of, 70
  stick and cope profiles, 57–59, 65
  styles, 56
  trash can, pull-out, 39–40, 140–142
  wall cabinet, number of doors for, 97, 98
Dovetail jig, 81
Dovetail joint, 77, 79, 81–83
Dowels, face frame, 50–51
Drawers, cabinet, 37–40, 74–83. *See also*
  Drawer-slide hardware
  attaching drawer fronts, 132–133
  basic drawer box, building, 78–80
  cutlist, 78
  design options, 56
  dimensions, 76, 78, 81
  dividers, 41, 138
  dovetailed drawers, 77, 79, 81–83
  face frame assembly, 45
  finishing, 76, 80, 82
  fronts, 64, 76–78, 83
  inset drawers, 52, 125
  joinery methods, 76–78, 81–83
  materials, 76–78
  pantry cabinet, 40
  plastic laminate lining, 78
  slide out trays, installation of, 124, 130
  style, 76–78
  trash can, pull-out, 39–40, 140–142
Drawer-slide hardware, 75, 78, 118, 128–130
  cost, 128
  inset drawers, hardware for, 125
  installing, 129–130
Drawings, design, 32–36
  cabinet size and location, 34–36
  plan and elevation, 34–36
Drill/driver
  corded, 16
  cordless, 14, 16, 102
Drill press, 11, 67
Driver. *See* Drill/driver
Drying of wood, 27–29
Drying rack, finish, 119

E

Electrical system, 32, 147
End panel cabinets
  base cabinets, 94–95
  refrigerator, 109
  solid wood end panels for, 41, 55, 71–73,
    94, 98
  wall cabinets, 97, 98, 103
End splits (lumber defect), 29
Engineered stone countertop, 157–160
Euro hinges, 124–127, 141
European-style cabinets, 37
Exotic wood, 24, 26

F

Face-frame construction, 42–53
    assembly, 47–53
    beaded frames, 51–53
    cabinet installation, adjustments for, 148
    corner cabinets, 49–50, 148
    dimensions, 44–47, 49
    inside corners, softening of, 50
    wood choice, 44
FAS grade, 27
FAS I-Face grade, 27
Fence
    chopsaw, 152
    drill press, 11
    rip, 9, 46, 89
    router, 65–67
Finishing, 112–121. See also Sanding
    after installation, 151
    door panels, 72
    drawers, 76, 80, 82
    drips, runs, and sags, avoiding, 116
    drying rack, 119
    kickspace trim, 151, 152
    safety, 115
    surface preparation, 114
    types of finishes, 115–121
Finish nailer, 79, 92
Fire prevention
    kitchen fire extinguisher, 38
    workshop, 16
Floor, 147
Frame-and-panel doors. See Doors, cabinet
Frame-and-panel drawer fronts, 64, 78, 83
Frame-and-panel end panels, 71–73
Frameless cabinets, 37

G

Glass-paneled doors, 41, 57, 62–63, 100
Glue
    application methods, 103
    base cabinets, 91
    doors, 70–72
    drawer, 83
    panels, 64
    removing, 60
    wall cabinets, 101, 103
Granite countertops, 160
Ground-fault circuit interrupters (GFCIs), 32

H

Hardware, 122–133
    concealed (Euro) hinges, 124–127, 141
    drawer-slide (See Drawer-slide hardware)
    knobs and pulls, 128, 131–132
    suppliers and manufacturers, 165
Hardwood, 24–26
    drawer boxes, 78
    grades, 27
    plywood veneers, 20–23
    raised panels, shaping, 67
    shelves, 104
Hickory, 26, 120
High-density fiberboard (HDF), 24
Honeycomb, 27
Hood, vent, 108
Humidity, reducing, 12, 26

I

Inset doors and doors
    beaded face frames for, 52
    hardware for, 125
Installation, 144–153
    base cabinets, 150–151
    plumb, level, and square, checking for,
        146–147

shimming, scribing, and trimming,
    147–150
studs, finding, 146
wall cabinets, 149
Island cabinets, 110–111

J

Jigs
    dovetail, 81
    pocket-hole, 14–15, 47–48, 78, 99
Jigsaw, 11, 67
Joiner, biscuit, 15, 90
Joinery methods. See also Biscuit joints
    angled joints, 98
    dovetail joints, 77, 79, 81–83
    drawers, 76–78, 81–83
    face frame, 47–48, 50–51
    frame-and-panel doors, 57
    locking-edge joints, 77
    locking-miter joints, 77
    mortise-and-tenon joints, 50
    pocket joinery (See Pocket holes/pocket
        joinery)
    rabbit and dado joints, 77
    wall cabinets, 98–101
Jointer, 10, 64
Jointing boards, 60

K

Kickspace trim, 88, 151–153
Knobs, 128, 131–132
Knots and knotholes, 29

L

Labeling parts, 98
Lacquer, 114
    brushing, 117–118
    nitrocellulose, 116–117
Laminate. See Plastic laminate
Layout tools, 17
Lazy Susans, 39, 50, 94, 102, 104, 126, 142–143
Level, checking for, 146–147
Level (tool), 17, 146
Light fixtures, 100, 147
Lineal foot (lf.), 22
Locking-edge joint, 77
Locking-miter joint, 77
Lumber. See Wood

M

Maple, 25, 27, 121
Medium-density fiberboard (MDF), 24
    as plywood core, 21–22
    shelves, 104
    templates, use for, 68
Melamine-coated particleboard (MCP), 23–24
Moisture content of wood, 27–29
Molding and trim
    crown molding, 36, 44, 151–153
    by lineal foot, 22
    T-molding, 136
Mortise-and-tenon joints, 50

N

Nailer, brad, 16–17
Nitrocellulose lacquer, 116–117
No. 1 Common grade, 27
No. 2 Common grade, 27

O

Oak, 25, 27, 120
Oil finishes, 114, 119, 120
Oil-varnish blend, shop-made, 119–121
Ovens, cabinets for wall, 109–110

P

Paint, 121
Panel cutter, 87
Panel layout software, 90
Panel saws, 9
Pantry cabinets, 40–41, 110
    dimensions, 108, 110
    end panels, 71–72
    top rail, width of, 44
Particleboard, 23–24
    as plywood core, 21–22
    shelves, 104
Pine, 26, 27, 78, 121
Plane, block, 148
Planer, 11, 14
Planing, 60, 64
Plastic edging, 136
Plastic laminate
    countertop, 156, 158–159, 162–163
    drawer lining, 78
Plate joiner, 15, 90
Plate joints. See Biscuit joints
Plumb, checking for, 146–147
Plumbing, 151
Plywood, 20–22
    Baltic-birch, 22, 76
    costs, 21
    cutting, 88, 89
    damage, protection from, 90
    dimensions, 76
    door panels, 56
    drawer boxes, 78
    grades, 23
    panel layout software, 90
    particleboard or MDF core, 21–22
    shelf edging for, 136–138
    shelves, 104, 137
    spacer blocks, 150
Pneumatic tools, 17, 79, 92
Pocket-hole jig, 14–15, 47–48, 78, 99
Pocket holes/pocket joinery, 42, 47–48, 50
    base cabinets, 90
    drawer, 78–79
    wall cabinets, 99–100
Polyurethane varnish, 114, 118–119
Poplar, 78
Pulls, 128, 131–132
Push sticks, 46

R

Rabbet and dado joint, 77
Rails
    end panels, 71
    face frame, 44–50
    frame-and-panel doors, 56–61, 64–65, 70
Random-orbit sander, 15–16, 57, 71, 114
Receptacles, 32, 147, 151
Records, project, 70
Refrigerator cabinets, 108–109
Resources, 165
Ring shake (ring failure), 27
Rip fence, 9, 46, 73, 89
Rollout shelves/trays, installation of, 124, 130,
    142
Rosettes, 73

Router bits, 56–58, 65
  cabinet doors, buying for, 59
  cleaning, 64
  flush-trim, 83
  lubricating bearings, 66
  raised panels, for, 57, 65–67
  safe use of, 58
  storage of, 70
Router/router table, 13
  drawers, grooving, 78
  raised panels, shaping, 65–67
  safe operation of, 57, 58

S
Safety
  cutting plywood, 89
  ear protection, 57
  finishing process, 115
  helper, use of, 26
  push sticks, use of, 46
  router, use of, 57, 58
  solvent-based contact cement, use of, 156
  tools, use of, 16
Sander, random-orbit, 15–16, 57, 71, 114
Sanding, 114
  doors, 67–71
  drawer boxes, 80, 83
  wall cabinets, 104
Sanding sponge, 67
Saw blades
  chopsaws, 10
  cleaning, 10
  combination, 9
  composite, 9
  DeWalt framing blade, 136
  extra-fine cutoff, 8, 89
  laminate cutting blade to cut composite panels, 24
  melamine, 8, 88
  table saw, 8, 9, 24, 88, 136
Saws. See also Chopsaws; Panel cutter; Table saw
  bandsaw, 11
  cabinet, 87
  circular, 89
  jigsaw, 11, 67
  panel, 9
  sliding compound-miter, 12
Scale, architect's, 34
Scribing, 147–149
Select grade, 27
Shaper cutter, 13, 56, 57, 65
Shellac, 119–120
Shelves
  edge treatment options, 136–138
  rollout, 124, 130, 142
  supports, 100–101
Shimming, 147–150
Sink base cabinets, 35
Sink trays, 140–141
Slideout shelves, 124, 130
Slide rule, shop-made, 60
Sliding compound-miter saws, 12
Soapstone countertops, 160
Soffits, 36
Software
  computer-aided design, 32–33, 165
  cutlist, 90
  panel layout, 90
Softwood, 24
  raised panels, shaping, 67
  types of, 26
Solid surface material countertop, 156–157
Solid wood, 19, 24–27. See also Hardwood
  countertop, 162
  door panels, 56

drawer fronts, 64, 76–78, 83
end panels (See End panel cabinets)
shelf edging, 136–138
Spaceballs™, 70
Spacer blocks, 150
Spray-finishing equipment, 17, 116–118
Squares, 17, 90
Stain, 121
Stainless steel countertop, 163
Steaming dents, 114
Stick and cope profiles, 58, 59, 65
Stickering lumber, 28–29
Stiles
  base cabinets, 90–91
  beveling for cabinet installation, 147–148
  end panels, 71–72
  face frame, 43–50
  frame-and-panel doors, 56–58, 60, 64–65, 70
  hinges, installation of, 126
  wall cabinets, 98, 103
Stone countertops
  engineered stone, 156–160
  granite, 160
Storage
  of lumber, 28–29
  of router bits, 70
Stove, wall cabinets above, 108
Studs, finding, 146
Supports, shelf, 100–101, 138–140
Surface checks (lumber defect), 29
Surface preparation, 114

T
Table saw, 8–9
  blade types, 8, 9, 24, 88, 136
  cutting panels on, 24
  fence (See fence)
  grooving drawers, 78
  mobile base for, 14
  outfeed table, 8–9, 17, 87, 89
  push sticks, use of, 46
  ripping face frame members on, 46
  sliding table, 9, 89
  waxing, 12
Tack cloth, 114
Tape measure, 17
Tearout, avoiding, 60
Thickness planer, 11, 14
Tile countertops, 160–162
T-molding, 136
Tools, 6–17. See also specific tools
  batteries for, 16
  electrical service for, 14
  layout, 17
  mobile base for, 14
  pneumatic, 17, 79, 92
  portable power tools and accessories, 13–17
  push sticks, 46
  rust, preventing, 12
  safe use, 16
  sources of, 165
  stationary machinery, 8–13
Trash can, pull-out, 39–40, 140–142
Trays, rollout, 124, 130, 142
Trays, storage of, 41
Trimming, 147–149
Twist (lumber defect), 29

V
Varnish
  conversion, 116
  oil-varnish blend, shop-made, 119–121
  polyurethane, 118–119
Vix bits, 127

W
Wall cabinets, 96–105
  assembling, 101–102
  corner cabinets, 97, 104–105
  cutlist, 98
  cutting and joinery details, 98–101
  dimensions and design options, 98
  doors, number of, 97, 98
  end panel cabinets, 97, 98, 103
  face frames (See Face-frame construction)
  finishing, 104
  installing, 36, 149
  recessed bottom panel, 99–100
  refrigerator, above, 108–109
  shelf supports, 100–101
  stove, above, 108
  top rail, width of, 44
  under-cabinet light fixtures, 100
  for wall ovens, 109–110
Wall ovens, cabinets for, 109–110
Warped boards, use of, 58
Wave (lumber defect), 29
White pine, 26
Wind (lumber defect), 29
Wine rack, 138
Wiring, 147
Wood, 18–29. See also Plywood; Solid wood
  composite-wood panels, 19–24
  defects, common, 29
  doors, for, 61
  drawers, for, 64, 76–78
  drying, issues of, 27–29
  face frame, for, 44
  grain orientation and wood movement, 29
  measurements, 22
  sources of, 20, 22, 27–28
  stickering, 28–29
  storage, 28–29
Wood conditioner, 121
Wood edge banding, 136–138
Wood filler, 116
Workbench, 17
Work triangle, 33

Y
Yellow pine, 26

Other Books in the Series

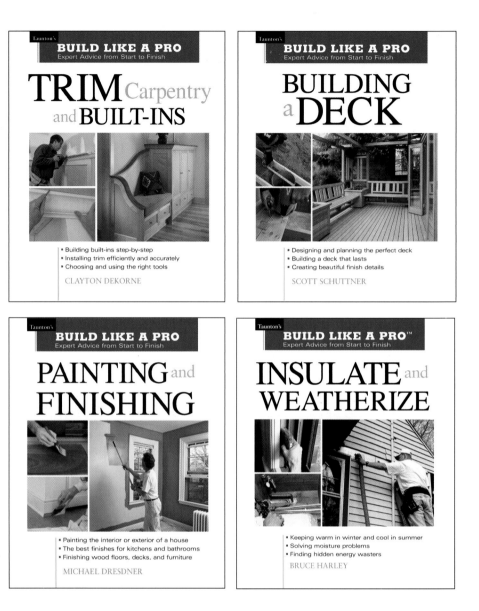

Taunton's BUILD LIKE A PRO
Expert Advice from Start to Finish

TRIM Carpentry and BUILT-INS

- Building built-ins step-by-step
- Installing trim efficiently and accurately
- Choosing and using the right tools

CLAYTON DEKORNE

Taunton's BUILD LIKE A PRO
Expert Advice from Start to Finish

BUILDING a DECK

- Designing and planning the perfect deck
- Building a deck that lasts
- Creating beautiful finish details

SCOTT SCHUTTNER

Taunton's BUILD LIKE A PRO
Expert Advice from Start to Finish

PAINTING and FINISHING

- Painting the interior or exterior of a house
- The best finishes for kitchens and bathrooms
- Finishing wood floors, decks, and furniture

MICHAEL DRESDNER

Taunton's BUILD LIKE A PRO™
Expert Advice from Start to Finish

INSULATE and WEATHERIZE

- Keeping warm in winter and cool in summer
- Solving moisture problems
- Finding hidden energy wasters

BRUCE HARLEY